CAMILLE

Camille

The Life of Camille Claudel, Rodin's Muse and Mistress

REINE-MARIE PARIS

TRANSLATED FROM THE FRENCH BY
LILIANE EMERY TUCK

SEAVER BOOKS

HENRY HOLT AND COMPANY

New York

Library of Congress Cataloging in Publication Data
Paris, Reine-Marie.
[Camille Claudel.   English]
Camille: the life of Camille Claudel, Rodin's muse and mistress
Reine-Marie Paris: translated from the French by Liliane Emery Tuck.—1st American ed.
p.   cm.
Translation of: Camille Claudel, 1864–1943.
Bibliography: p.
1. Claudel, Camille, 1864–1943.   2. Sculptors—France—Biography.
3. Mistresses—France—Biography.   4. Rodin, Auguste, 1840–1917—
Relations with women.   I. Title.
NB553.C44P313 1988
730'.92'4—dc19
[B]   87–28550
ISBN 0–8050–0582–X   CIP

All photographs are by Anne Schaeffer with the exception of the following:
Frontispiece, 1, anonymous; 2, Chéron; 4, anonymous; 7, 9, Reine-Marie Paris; 12, 14, 16, 17,
55, 56, 65, 113, Bruno Jarret—ADAGP and Musée Rodin by SPADEM; 20–27, Bibliothèque
Nationale, Paris; 29, 30, anonymous; 33, Jessie Lipscomb, courtesy of her grandson; 34–37,
Reine-Marie Paris; 91, 92, Musée d'Art et d'Histoire, Geneva; 95, Pierre et Françoise Bouchez.

Frontispiece: Camille Claudel by César, 1884.

First American Edition

Designed by Susan Hood
Printed in the United States of America
10 9 8 7 6 5 4 3 2 1

ISBN 0-8050-0582-X

TO MY FAMILY

Contents

Illustrations follow pages 22, 86, and 176.

Introduction

The Fortunes and Misfortunes of a Destiny and a Work

If I am born for the sake of duty, God should then remove from my head the love of art, poetry and the instinct for freedom which turn my duties into torments and an agony; should I be born for the sake of art and liberty, he should remove from my heart pity, friendship, solicitude and the fear of causing suffering which will always poison my triumphs and impede my career.

George Sand, *Consuelo*

In 1884, the photographer César captured with a masterful click the imperious Camille Claudel, in the glory of her twentieth year and at the outset of her career. As a young girl, she was no ordinary or passive beauty—her attractiveness already held a promise. The frontispiece shows us the portrait of a conqueror whose will to live and whose will to create dominate her expression.

Only the woman's destiny did not fulfill the superb young girl's promise; it was a disaster. And yet, at first, she was fortunate: Camille had talent, intelligence and courage. She was helped by lucky coincidences that opened doors and blazed a trail for her artistic career. Her parents were not uncooperative. She had excellent teachers—one of whom was incomparable and more than just a teacher. But she collapsed. Struck down by a vertigo, she sank into a stupor and a darkness then, virtually unknown.

ix

Camille Claudel died legally in 1943 at the age of seventy-nine, but by 1910 she was already dead to society and to art. Her brief career was stamped with signs of lack of achievement and a paralysis before a goal never realized. Her life, like those of such hapless artists as Rimbaud and Van Gogh, takes on the mythic proportions of our modern-day heroes.

Camille Claudel's name and work are, for the most part, unfamiliar to the average visitor to museums and exhibitions. Her work, like the small tributary of a large river that loses its way in the sand, is barely distinguishable from the work of Auguste Rodin, while her name has been absorbed by that of her brother, the poet and playwright Paul Claudel, and his prolific genius and fame covered and smothered her like volcanic ash. Her first name, too—Camille, asexual in French—helped to condemn her to indetermination, the mother of forgetfulness.

Posterity has yet to make amends to Camille Claudel for her misfortunes. At the end of her solitary and miserable life, she left a sparse and nearly forgotten body of work, some resting in the shadow of Rodin's, the rest scattered and neglected in small provincial museums, in storage or perhaps in private and uncataloged collections. Several of her works have disappeared without leaving a trace; unless they resurface by chance, the loss seems all the more poignant, considering how very briefly she worked and how very little she left us.

If one had to name not a culprit—as did Paul Claudel in his grief and distaste for the squalid existence of his sister—but a catalyst for so many of her misfortunes, it would have to be Rodin. Rodin gave nearly everything to Camille Claudel and, at the same time, took it all away. The nature of the tragedy of this unfinished work and this fractured life lies in the failure of an ambivalent relationship that was reciprocally both fecund and destructive.

The work of Camille Claudel attests to the desperate effort of the disciple who tries to escape the influence of the master not so much by a break or a disavowal but by a deeper and more concentrated form. But while she was straining to achieve this and creating her purest masterpieces, Rodin, her teacher, rejected her and forced her to make the break. The effect of Rodin's abandonment on Camille Claudel's life can be compared to a huge geological split that swallowed up her creative sources. It was as if, all of a sudden, her inspiration had been denied her. Doubting more and more in herself, her art, art itself, she withdrew into silence—not a silence of mockery as did some of her contemporaries but a silence of unreason.

The end of her artistic life is the double darkness and the reality of Balzac's *Chef-d'oeuvre inconnu* (*The Unknown Masterpiece*), where the hero dies in absolute solitude. Beauty too closely espied fled from him and he disappeared, managing only to paint his ideal model's foot drowned in a chaos of color. It is a troubling precursor: before darkness totally engulfed her, Camille Claudel modeled only disembodied hands and feet.

Unhappy artist, romantic figure, nothing is missing in Camille Claudel's life to capture our interest today. In addition, her story should hold our attention because it is one of a woman who died trying, too soon, to escape the feminine condition. And if her suffering was caused by a man, is that not proof that she was excessively feminine? She was so, moreover, during a time when to be anything but wife, mother or nun was forbidden. Her background could not compensate for this "original sin"—there was no family fortune to provide her with studios and models, to subsidize a pleasant, sociable life similar to the ones of a few forgotten celebrities. There was no artistic environment that would lead her to L'École des Beaux-Arts or—and why not?—to the Prix de Rome. All of that was closed to a woman. Provincial and without connections and support, she could not help but become completely dependent on her teacher in exchange for the gift she made of herself. This exchange was the secret of her genius. When it dissolved, everything crumbled.

Yet Camille Claudel is with us still.

If one appreciates sculpture, a perhaps more difficult art, one has to recognize the magnitude of Rodin's output. And in so doing, one cannot help but notice—with delight—the transition from *The Thinker* (*Le Penseur*) to *Thought* (*La Pensée*)—a luminous and at once carnal manifestation of the passage of that free spirit—one could almost say a trace of a wild beast—which is what Camille Claudel was in late-nineteenth-century French sculpture. This young woman is the irruption in sculpture of that vague emotion, both tender and sad, a new expression, her expression in *Thought*—one of powerful inward force as well as of passion.

Why then should we be astonished that the marriage of this inwardness and intensity could animate such overt sensuality? It is clear that Camille's intimacy with Rodin opened the doors onto the "flesh," admitted and incorporated it into works that until then were fairly austere, obsessed with athletes, energetic hikers, weighty shades, and by women, the woman Eve who does not dare look at her own body. The apparition of this delicate carnality, of this nimble sensuality, wrought out of twining limbs, the play of skin textures and of couples attentive only to each other is characteristic of the works of Rodin from 1883 to 1890 and is the reflection of Camille Claudel. How can one escape the seduction of *Eternal Springtime* (*L'Éternel printemps*), of *Eternal Idol* (*L'Éternelle idole*), that ballet of fauns and nymphs whose charms and grace find no equal in the sculpture of the period and founded no school—except for a few Art Nouveau works unfortunately devalued by the fashion of the times? How also can one resist the seduction of Camille Claudel's masterpiece, *The Abandonment* (*Çacountala*) and perhaps the fulfillment of that style? But the expression of barely veiled desire on Rodin's part became, in the work of Camille Claudel, a contained emotion, full of spiritual significance. Subjectivity no longer resided in the glance of the observer but was embodied in the figures themselves. At its apogee, the art of Camille Claudel generates a light, a breath, a feeling of balance that only a woman of genius could achieve. And, after all, wasn't this rediscovery of equilibrium a reaction of Rodin's disciples to their master's obsession with motion? But in his only female disciple there is more: there is this gold Rodin flattered himself to have found in her, and like a clever goldsmith he knew how to use it for himself.

It is time for this gold to shine and time, in fact, to resolve the contradictions of a life, to value the originality of a work that has all the characteristics of greatness. Now, especially, when we are so concerned with repairing the injustices done to our forebears and reclaiming what was lost, we must reestablish Camille Claudel among the great French sculptors of the past.

The fame of Giorgione, a painter of genius—a parallel that will illustrate these preliminary ideas—was for a long period eclipsed by that of Titian, and the merit of his work fluctuated according to the whims of art historians, either to the profit or to the detriment of the great Venetian. Camille Claudel is a sort of Giorgione in relation to Rodin. Just as it has been difficult to delineate the parameters of the master of Castelfranco from those of his famous teacher, so it will be no easy matter to disentangle Camille Claudel from her celebrated master, to show her originality, her secret influence, or to actually separate her work from Rodin's. But during the course of research, what a joy to discover new areas that are still intact! In Camille Claudel's case, however, so close to us in time and space, this effort is particularly awkward. Jealousy and indifference, which Camille believed herself to be the victim of—often wrongly—have accomplished their task of disorder and destruction and followed her to the grave.

A few years before Camille Claudel's death, Jacques Cassar, the historian, with all the love associated with a long friendship, knew better than anyone else how to plead Camille's case, and he addressed his text to the author of this work.

Convinced as I am that there is no better prelude to the pages that follow, I cannot resist the temptation of reproducing it in its entirety with my posthumous thanks for his advice and the "viaticum" he gave me at the start of this complicated journey which is the biography of Camille Claudel.

A PLEA FOR CAMILLE CLAUDEL

No one today disputes the genius of [Paul] Claudel nor that of Rodin, whose names, like their works, have acquired a universal dimension. Does it follow then that Camille Claudel's sole merit was to have been the sister of one and the student—or the lover—of the other? That injustice we must now repair.

Already great before her meeting with Rodin, Camille Claudel managed by 1895 to impose her work, if not, alas, on the amateurs, at least on the experienced critics who never spared her their admiration.

"A revolt against nature: a woman of genius," wrote Mirbeau.

Mathias Morhardt finishes his remarkable study which he devoted to her thus: "In 1889, she works. Independent of the clamor that may arise around her, she thinks only about sculpture. . . . She goes on! She belongs to the race of heroes!" And in 1907, Charles Morice, Gauguin's friend, sets up a shout—too late—that was lost in indifference: "The talent of Camille Claudel is one of the glories at the same time that it is one of the shames of our country."

She, of whom Rodin had said, "I showed her where she could find gold but the gold she finds belongs to her," had by 1906 ceased all creative activity.

She was locked up in 1913 and, after thirty years of seclusion, died on October 19, 1943, in the asylum of Montdevergues.

She leaves us a work stamped with the seal of exemplariness: small but of a quality that makes it equal to the works of the greatest sculptors, beginning with Rodin.

Such undeniable masterpieces as *Bust of Rodin* (*Buste de Rodin*), *The Abandonment* (*Çacountala*), *The Waltz* (*La Valse*), *Clotho*, *The Gossipers* (*Les Causeuses*), *The Wave* (*La Vague*) or *Maturity* (*L'Age mûr*) are sufficient to establish the glory of Camille Claudel.

Camille Claudel Statuary

Statues, liberated from obelisk and term, standing in the agora of ancient Greece—these were true bodies of men and women, enduring standards of canonical being. These immortal inhabitants were made of the very stone of which the city is built. Gods, heroes, victors in the games, they offer to those passing by the motionless image of that perfect person the crowd animates, distorts, multiplies. Naked, they stand—on their own feet. They are the splendid growth of the free creature in all its columnar integrity. They possess their harmony complete in themselves; visible from all sides, they turn with the eyes, and with the light that turns around them. These shafts, aloft all day long, mark out aerial space and comprise the monument of the site. Wherever the light takes them, it finds there the whole person, alive.

But when the Word of Christ destroyed, with silence, the scattered expectation of the gods whom man had elected to keep it for him, this fictive people, along with the actual one, was convoked from streets and squares to the sacramental gathering; they enter and incorporate themselves into the Church. The individual body is no longer self-sufficient—its value is granted now by the place it occupies and by the gesture or the sign it makes, and not by what it is, but by what it says. And of the sun it espouses only certain rays at certain times. At its post in the Gospel, like the priest and the flock, like the candle and the bell, the stone saint or the stone demon discharges this task according to the Canonical Hour.

Then, after long centuries of discipline and hierarchy, when the statue on the walls of convent or town hall, sign, emblem and ensign within the gable of the Goldsmiths' or Leather Workers' Guild, stands its official ground, Society, hitherto confined to the ramparts of the keep and the alleyways of the town, opens to daylight its windows and doors. The narrow loophole is transformed into the high casement, and it becomes necessary to arrange the vassal bit of earth now evident to the eye, for the eye's delight. So for three centuries art concerns itself with the deployment of façades and gardens, what beholds and what is beheld. The medieval statue was created for its role in the total stone, this one for its position in the decor. But, as in the preceding ages, the statue still fulfills, still establishes the governing attitude. Among an architecture of palaces and fountains, it calmly triumphs over the spectacle so magnificently disposed round about; and, towering over mausoleums now, it measures the avenues of life. The hosts of Fable and the Past are released from woods and mists to pay their homage to the lord of the place; he recognizes them before his eyes as in his memory— how agreeably they accompany him! They illuminate the site. And a thicket thus becomes the grove of Mercury or Apollo. And still the rampart, the screen of galleries and quincunxes, the play of drapery offer the stroller no more than the welcoming gesture prepared for him by the spy stationed in his path.

In the nineteenth century, the context of life loses its fixity, its hierarchies; demarcation becomes impossible, and the need vanishes to embellish it, to accommodate its perpetually renewed field. Along with the lord of the manor, the god disappears from his gardens. The mob scatters its own vague idols over precarious tribunals: Justice, Electricity, Raspail. Everywhere, melancholy men in modern dress stain their cheap limestone pedestals with green juice. And as for naked women, the woeful crew of sculptors continues to hew them out for interment in cemeteries and museums. Our own day bears witness to the paroxysm and the agony of this art.

Must we then assume that by dint of frequenting tombs, sculpture today is so dead an art that it has lost its very reason for being? Not so.

xvi

Sculpture expresses the need to touch. Even before he can see, the child waves his tiny swarming hands about. The almost maternal joy of possessing the plastic earth between his hands, the art of modeling, of possessing— henceforth enduringly between his ten fingers—these full forms, these splendid living machines he sees moving around him: it is for these that desire first appears in him, satisfied by the first arch and the first doll. But, henceforth proscribed from public square and open air, sculpture, like the other arts, withdraws into that solitary room where the poet shelters his forbidden dreams.

Camille Claudel is the first practitioner of this interior sculpture.

Every room is a kind of huge secret in which whatever daylight it admits undergoes an occult decantation. Here the play of the sun's rays penetrates only obliquely, for a few hours, if the overcast skies of our climate permit even so much. The room takes only a diminished light from the day; it is filled with lucent air between its papered walls, as a glass is filled with water. All the hours, all the accidents of the sky are disclosed by an exquisite decrepitude of this interior and inhabited atmosphere. A cavity is modeled as though by the use of our own body. The thousand objects adorning it—furniture, chandeliers, mirrors—appropriate the ambient brightness to themselves, and from the contrasted interplay of shadows and reflections, sensitive to the finest relaxations of the imprisoned singing hour, decompose its harmony. Since each has value only by our use of it, all become a persistent expression of ourselves: whence the touching character is assumed, in this room where the beloved no longer exists, by that gleam of the mirror, that hat on the open piano, that bouquet of leaves and flowers in the mystery of the orange evening.

Unobservant critics have frequently compared Camille Claudel's art to that of a sculptor I shall not name.[*] As a matter of fact, a more complete and flagrant antithesis is unthinkable: the art of that sculptor is the heaviest, the most material there is; indeed, certain of his figures cannot release themselves from the clay in which they are enmeshed. When they do not crawl, embracing the mud in a kind of erotic frenzy, it seems as if each of these embracing bodies is trying to return to the primal lump. On all sides,

[*] Alas, I am nonetheless compelled to acknowledge that Rodin was an artist of genius. (1928)

impenetrable and compact, the group resists the light, like a boundary stone. In short, peasant work, served by a devious mind and ill-served by a naturally glum and impoverished imagination.

The art of Camille Claudel, from the first, glistens with the characteristics that are peculiarly its own: here we see the most powerful and the most naïve imagination taking its magnificent way—it is the gift of invention. Her genius is that of the things she is appointed to represent. The sculptural object, for her, is what has become capable of being detached, what can be gathered up and possessed between intelligent hands. The things whose uninterrupted whole constitutes the spectacle we observe are animated by various movements whose composition at certain solemn moments of duration, in a sort of lyric ejaculation, invents a kind of common figure, a precarious and multiple being. It is this new and composite being, this key to an assemblage of movements, which we call the *motif*. Thus like a sigh that ends in a cry, the joy of the June meadow somehow explodes in an enthusiastic flower! A tree cut down, the rebel on his barricade, a wild horse mastered, the murderer threatening his wife with a hoe—so many knots and reductions, so many suddenly intelligible keys to a multitude of movements and comparisons, behind, around, within the world and our minds. It is such *finds* that well up, as though from the very ground of nature, from a poet's heart: we see them incarnated in the work of Camille Claudel with a kind of ingenuous joy, forming, in all the meanings of these adjectives, the world's most "animated" and most "spiritual" art.

While a figure by that other sculptor remains closed and inert beneath the sunbeam that tinges it, a group by Camille Claudel is always open and filled with the breath that has "inspired" it. The former repulses light; the latter, in the center of the chiaroscuro room, welcomes it, just as a splendid bouquet would do. Sometimes, with the most amusing caprice, the honeycombed figure divides and differentiates the light, like a stained-glass window. Sometimes, by the profound harmony of the highlights and shadows it encloses, the concave figure acquires a kind of resonance and descant. I shall instance only a few of the famous pieces: *Fortune;* the marble from *The Abandonment* (*Çacountala*), this year's Salon; so euphoric that, like skin itself, it delights the hands with the eye; *Clotho,* a kind of dreadful distaff hidden in the wool of her fatal locks; the drunken *Waltz*

(*La Valse*), shaken and lost in the very fabric of the music, in the storm and whirlwind of the dance; *The Gossipers* (*Les Causeuses*); *The Wave* (*La Vague*), which huddle beneath the huge breaking wave; finally *Maturity* (*L'Age mûr*), in which the movement is created by garments, by the ground itself, by a kind of fatal power that compels the actors to their places by the omnipresent obligation of the oblique generatrix, who, wresting man from the hands of youth, drags him toward his fate, pasted against the wizened womb of a grinning and lubricious old age. Drapery, in Camille Claudel's work, takes something of the role of Wagnerian recitative which, adopting, enveloping, developing the theme, constitutes its unity within the total radiance.

Just as a man sitting in the countryside employs, to accompany his meditation, a tree or a rock on which to anchor his eye, so a work by Camille Claudel in the middle of a room is, by its mere form, like those curious stones the Chinese collect: a kind of monument of inner thought, the tuft of a theme accessible to any and every dream. While a book, for example, must be taken from the shelves of our library, or a piece of music must be performed, the worked metal or stone here releases its own incantation, and our chamber is imbued with it.

Paul Claudel, 1905

Translated by Richard Howard

Acknowledgments

Without the encouragement and help of my friends, this work would never have seen the light of day. I wish to express my gratitude to them.

My thanks to the Claudel family for always guiding and sustaining me.

I also owe my gratitude to Professor François Lhermitte, to Dr. Jean-François Allilaire and to Mr. Bernard Howells, without whose collaboration two essential chapters on Camille Claudel could not have been written.

Special thanks to Mr. Maurice Coutot, genealogist, who enabled me to track down several collectors who either owned or had once owned works by the artist. Thanks to him and to Mr. Jean G. Marais, I discovered lost works and hope to find still more.

To accomplish this task and make the necessary corrections, I had the privilege of receiving the help of Mr. Gilbert Gadoffre and Mr. Michel Malicet, both eminent scholars of the work of Paul Claudel.

I am beholden to Mr. Bernard Dorival, who guided my first studies of Camille Claudel and who initiated me to research techniques.

I also want to thank the curators of the libraries and museums who facilitated my access to their archives and gave me their advice. In particular, Mrs. Florence Callu, chief curator of the Manuscript Department of the Bibliothèque Nationale; Mr. François Chapon, chief curator of the Bibliothèque Littéraire Jacques Doucet; Mrs. Monique Laurent, curator of the Musée Rodin; Miss Gisèle Chovin, curator of the Musée Bertrand Chateauroux; and Miss Francine Legrand, curator of the Musée Royal d'Art Moderne in Brussels.

I also wish to thank the following persons who helped me in various ways: Sister Saint Hubert from the Congregation of Saint-Charles; Mrs. Solange Seznec, co-director and in charge of administrative services at the Montfavet Hospital; Mrs. Nicole du Castel, Paul Dubois's granddaughter; Mrs. Suzanne Mulsant; the Philippe de Massary family; François de Massary; and the Maigret family.

Finally, I wish to thank Mrs. Jeanine Fricker and Mr. Pascal Fouché of the Editions Gallimard for their participation and their understanding.

Reine-Marie Paris

Chronology

1864   December 8: Birth of Camille Claudel, the daughter of Louis-Prosper Claudel, the registrar of mortgages in the town of Fère in the province of Tardenois (Aisne), and of Louise-Athanaïse Cerveaux, the daughter of Athanase Cerveaux, a doctor in Fère.

1865   January 25: Baptism by Nicolas Cerveaux, the pastor of the village of Villeneuve-sur-Fère and the uncle of Louise Claudel.

1866   February 26: Birth of Louise Claudel.

1868   August 6: Birth of Paul Claudel.

1869   The Claudel family moves to Bar-le-Duc (Meuse). Camille is taught by the Sisters of Christian Doctrine.

1876–
1879   Louis-Prosper Claudel is named the registrar of mortgages at Nogent-sur-Seine (Aube).

The Claudel children continue their studies under the direction of their tutor, M. Colin.

Camille molds her first figurines out of clay: *Bismarck* and *Napoleon I, David and Goliath.*

Alfred Boucher, the talented sculptor from Nogent, notices the little girl's talent.

1879–
1881   Louis-Prosper is transferred to Wassy-sur-Blaise (Haute-Marne).

1881   Arrival of Mme. Claudel and her children in Paris. They move into 135 bis Boulevard du Montparnasse. *Paul Claudel at Thirteen Years of Age* or *Young Roman* (plaster).
Paul is enrolled in the Lycée Louis-le-Grand.
Camille attends the Colarossi Academy and rents a studio at 117 rue Notre-Dame-des-Champs with some young English women.

1882   Alfred Boucher introduces Camille to Paul Dubois, the director of l'Ecole Nationale des Beaux-Arts.
Old Helen or *Bust of an Old Woman* (terra cotta).

1883   Louis-Prosper is transferred to Rambouillet.
Bust of a Woman (*Portrait of Madame B.*) (plaster). Private collection.

1884   *Young Roman* (*My Brother at Sixteen*) (plaster).
Sea Foam (marble and onyx).
Bust of Louis-Prosper Claudel; disappeared.
Rodin, replacing Alfred Boucher, apprentices Camille to his studio at 182 rue de l'Université.
Young Roman (the original plaster is tinted).
Torso of an Old Woman Standing (bronze).

1885   The Claudel family moves to 31 Boulevard de Port Royal.
Camille spends her vacations with her family in the Vosges and brings back some drawings.
Bust of Louise Claudel (terra cotta).
Giganti (bronze).

1886   A trip to the Isle of Wight with her brother, Paul, in the autumn.
Exhibition in Nottingham with her friend and studio partner, Jessie Lipscomb.

Portrait of Jessie Lipscomb (terra cotta).
Man Leaning (plaster).

1887   Louis-Prosper is transferred to Compiègne.
Portrait of Rodin Reading a Book (oil); disappeared.
Portrait of Maria Paillette (oil).
Louise Claudel (pastel).
Eugénie Plé (oil); disappeared.
Portrait of Victoire Joséphine Brunet (oil); disappeared.
A trip to Touraine with Rodin.

1888   Marriage of Louise Claudel to Ferdinand de Massary, a magistrate,
on August 16.
Rodin rents a studio, La Folie Neubourg, a dilapidated eighteenth-
century building at 68 Boulevard d'Italie, so that he can work
there with Camille.
Meets Claude Debussy.
Çacountala (plaster); honorable mention at the Salon des Artistes
Français.
Torso of a Crouching Woman (bronze).
Paul Claudel (pastel).
Ferdinand de Massary (bronze bust).
Bust of Rodin (bronze).
Trip to the Isle of Wight with Jessie Lipscomb.

1889   *Charles Lhermitte as a Child* (bronze bust).
Psalm; also called *The Prayer* (bronze bust).
Rodin, a founding member of La Société Nationale des Beaux-
Arts.

1890   Trip with Rodin to Touraine and Anjou.
Sojourn at the Château de l'Islette near Azay-le-Rideau.

1892   First study for *The Waltz* (plaster).
Rents a studio on the Boulevard d'Italie.

1893   Trip to Touraine.
The Waltz (life-size plaster).

Clotho (plaster).

Becomes a member of the Société Nationale des Beaux-Arts.

The Little Chatelaine (plaster).

1894   Sojourn to Guernsey.

The Painter (bronze); disappeared.

The Vanished God (plaster).

The Gossipers (plaster).

Trip to Touraine.

1895   State commission for *Maturity* (first version).

Commission for *Clotho* in marble to commemorate the Puvis de Chavannes dinner.

1896   Meets Mathias Morhardt, editor of the newspaper *Le Temps* and her first biographer.

November 20: death of Ferdinand de Massary, brother-in-law of Camille.

Marble bust of *The Little Chatelaine*.

Exhibits a *Waltz* (oxidized stoneware) at the Salon de l'Art Nouveau in Samuel Bing's gallery.

1897   Exhibits *Hamadryad* (marble and bronze) at Samuel Bing's gallery, rue de Provence; disappeared.

The Wave or *Bathers* (plaster).

Clotho or *The Fate* (marble).

1898   Rents a studio at 63 rue de Turenne.

Definite break with Rodin.

Death of a Little Girl with Doves (oil on canvas).

Second version of *Maturity* (plaster).

1899   Rents a studio at 19 Quai Bourbon.

Resigns from the Société Nationale des Beaux-Arts.

Deep in Thought or *Woman Seated Before a Hearth* (bronze and onyx).

Count Christian de Maigret in the Costume of Henry II (marble).

Perseus and the Gorgon (life-size plaster); disappeared.
Maturity (plaster—second project).

1900   Exhibits three works at the Universal Exposition.
Meets Eugène Blot, who will become her editor and friend.

1900?   *Woman on the Sofa* (oil on canvas).

1902   *The Alsatian Woman* (three-quarters life-size—terra cotta with a silver patina); disappeared.
Portrait of the Countess de Maigret (marble).
Refuses to exhibit in Prague with Rodin.

1903   *Maturity* (bronze).

1905   Trip to the Pyrenees with her brother and some friends.
Paul Claudel writes "Camille Claudel Statuary," published in the magazine *l'Occident,* and "Rodin, or the Man of Genius," which remains unpublished until the publication of Volume 18 of his complete works (Gallimard).
Çacountala (bronze).
The Flute Player or *The Siren* (bronze).
Bust of Paul Claudel at Thirty-seven Years (plaster).
Vertumnus and Pomona (*Çacountala*) (marble).
Perseus and the Gorgon (bronze).
Aurora (marble).
Dream by the Fire or *Woman Seated Before a Hearth* (marble).
Exhibition at the Eugène Blot gallery.

1906   Beginning of her madness.
The Wounded Niobide (bronze) commissioned by the state.

1908   Exhibition at the Eugène Blot gallery.

1910   *Bust of Paul Claudel at Forty-two Years of Age* (bronze).

1913   March 2: death of Louis-Prosper Claudel in Villeneuve-sur-Fère.
March 10: committed to the psychiatric hospital at Ville-Évrard.
July: a special issue of *l'Art décoratif* is dedicated to Camille

Claudel and includes Paul Claudel's article "Camille Claudel Statuary."

1914   August: Camille Claudel is transferred to Enghien, then to Montdevergues, near Avignon.

1929   June 20: death of Louise-Athanaïse Claudel.

1935   May 3: death of Louise de Massary.

1943   October 19: Camille Claudel dies at Montdevergues.

NOTE: Only the most important works have been cited in this chronology.

CAMILLE

Chapter 1

Fragments of a Biography:
Childhood and Adolescence (1864-1882)

Look at how lovely she is, oh, you can't imagine how lovely; . . .
But what is loveliest about her is her hair, red as gold.

Paul Claudel, *L'Endormie*

While the work of Camille Claudel is fragmentary and half forgotten, the events of her life are also clouded in obscurity. We have a few salient details, a few images culled from the life of her brother, but the thread that binds them often escapes us.

A large part of her correspondence has disappeared, notably the letters she wrote to her father and to Rodin,* to whom, we know, she bared her soul. She had few friends and rarely did she confide in them—a symptom of her withdrawal which, with time, grew fiercer and ended in prostration. Her mental illness, the catastrophe of her life, remains to this day an unexplored mystery. In short, an attempt to reconstitute the life of Camille Claudel would require the investigation of a detective and the patience of

---

*In the archives of the Rodin Museum, among a few salvaged letters, there exists a large envelope that bears Rodin's handwriting—"Camille Claudel Case"—but the envelope is empty. It is tempting to believe, as Camille did, in a conspiracy launched against her in her lifetime that followed her into the grave.

1

an archivist. In fact, Jacques Cassar, after years of research and thought, admitted to being a long way away from discovering the key to that solitary and secret life.

A small village situated between Soissons and Reims, Villeneuve-sur-Fère, has no particular signs or historical monuments to attract the casual visitor. Eight kilometers away, Fère is a large, dull market town, the center of the Tardenois district, in turn, the heart of France. Albeit austere, this land of rolling hills is not devoid of a certain appeal. No longer the decorous "île de France," these are the windswept rainy foothills of the Champagne district where Camille Rosalie Claudel was born on December 8, 1864.

The Champenoise Camille Claudel was a native of a land already rich with writers. Their names ring out with a flourish—La Fontaine, Racine, Alexander Dumas—rich, too, with the many anonymous sculptors whose works adorn Reims and Troyes and whose delicate elegant statuary embellishes and glorifies the countryside. Likewise, the art of Paul and Camille Claudel would continue that tradition and extend the glory of Champagne well into the middle of the present century.

The Claudel family was by no means rich. They were an old established bourgeois family that dated from the seventeenth century. Louis-Prosper, Camille's father, came from Bresse, near Gerardmer, and, in the summers, he liked to return there with his family. Although educated by the Jesuits in Strasbourg, he was said to be a Freemason. He finished school with an armful of prizes and became a registrar of mortgages. He held a variety of posts before he was finally allocated to Fère-en-Tardenois in 1860. In 1862, he married Louise Cerveaux.

It was Louise who was from Champagne and it was she who provided the family house in Villeneuve. She moored the Claudel family to the land she was said to resemble: "A humble and undemanding woman, she acted like a downtrodden peasant, a little like Elizabeth in *L'Annonce faite à Marie* with a bit of Colette's Sido thrown in."[*] Louise also brought inherited land and respectability from her side of the family, the Thierrys. Her father was a well-known doctor; her brother, Nicolas Cerveaux, was the abbot of Villeneuve. The union of Louise and Louis-Prosper marked their entrance into bourgeois life, and in Villeneuve they ruled like squires. They had

---

[*] Louis Chaigne, *La Vie de Paul Claudel* (Tours: Mame, 1962), page 21.

2

three surviving children (the oldest, Henri, died in infancy): Camille; Louise, born in 1866; and Paul, born in 1868.

Little is known of Camille Claudel's early years in Villeneuve and later, after 1870, in Bar-le-Duc, to which the family repaired in the winter. But the climate and especially the family atmosphere were hardly conducive to a happy childhood. The writer Henri Guillemin suggests that the whole Claudel family behaved in an arrogant fashion on the strength of their mystical and quite unassailable faith in their own superiority[*] while Paul Claudel compared the ambiance at Villeneuve to that of *Wuthering Heights*. Apparently the house raged and "everyone always fought in the family."[†]

Louis-Prosper kept his good manners for the outside world and allowed his bad temper to reign at home. He was not a mean man at heart. He had the bourgeois virtues and a deep-seated respect for money. Nothing angered him quite so much as extravagance, which, in his own words, was "the fruit of disorder and misdeed." But he was not a miser. He did not hesitate to sell his holdings when it was time for the family to move to Paris or to help his eldest daughter. Although authoritarian, he was not a tyrant. In matters that counted, he was never to oppose the heretical vocations of his children—a rather remarkable attitude for a provincial functionary. His letters to his son concerning his early works are astonishingly apt, and he accepted his eldest daughter's dedication not to the household but to the arts—he even facilitated the first steps in Camille's career.

Louise Claudel, on the other hand, never really loved or understood her temperamental daughter. She was completely blind to art, and it was obvious that she preferred her younger daughter, Louise, who remained obediently at her side. Later, Louise would never forgive Camille her dissipated way of life. Luckily, she never had the power to smother Camille's nascent talent or to thwart her formation.

As a result, the Claudel children grew up in such a highly charged and emotionally arid environment that their affective faculties seemed forever repressed. The father's volatile temper was never effectively balanced by a mother's tenderness and love, so deeply was Louise rooted in her rigid principles and submission.

No doubt Camille was perceived as a spirited and at times violent young

[*] Henri Guillemin, *Le Converti Paul Claudel* (Paris: Gallimard, 1968), page 44.
[†] Paul Claudel, *Mémoires improvisés* (Paris: Gallimard, 1969), pages 13, 19.

woman as well as an unusually beautiful one. The famous preface Paul Claudel wrote for the catalog of his sister's exhibit in 1951 testifies to that: "I see her once again as she was, a superb young woman, triumphant in her beauty and genius, wielding an often cruel ascendancy over my early years."[*] The word "superb" recurs like a leitmotif in the descriptions of Camille, and certainly she must have been arrogant. Already, as a child, she had no doubts about her talent.

The intimacy between brother and sister has aroused a lot of curiosity and speculation. The flame of genius in Paul is said to have been lit by Camille and their unshakable conviction in their work has been attributed to mutual emulation. Their relationship might interest psychiatrists who have used it to better understand the poet but, to this day, that sort of analysis has been unable to reveal much about the sculptor. It is a fact that Camille deeply loved her brother. The last words on her lips before she died were "My little Paul." But that this affection was the motivating force behind her artistic endeavor seems a very remote possibility. She had begun to work with clay as a small child, and no single event or influence can be attributed to that already passionate activity. Sculpture consumed her and drew in everyone around her—her father, her mother, her brother and sister; all had to pose for her even before she had taken a single lesson.[†]

In a rather mystical fashion, Camille was also attracted to nature. Her favorite walk with Paul was close to Villeneuve. The Geyn (a perverted form of the French word *géant*) was a sinister moor whose horizon was outlined by strange huge rocks, like petrified giants. Who could doubt that these stones modeled by the gods did not inspire the child, Camille, in much the same way that she must have inspired little Paul? Much later, he was to place his Violaine in the desert, Violaine who is Camille's avatar, her double and her opposite, and who likewise, frustrated in her role as wife and mother, succumbs under the weight of her destiny.

In 1869, Louis-Prosper was promoted and the Claudels established their residence in Bar-le-Duc. Camille became a student of the Sisters of Christian

---

[*] Paul Claudel, *L'Oeil écoute* (Paris: Gallimard, 1964), page 20. (Quoted in Bernard Champigneulle, *Rodin*, tr. J. Maxwell Brownjohn [London: Thames and Hudson, 1967].
[†] Mathias Morhardt, "Mlle. Camille Claudel," *Mercure de France,* March 1898, page 910.

Doctrine. Then, in 1876, Louis-Prosper was sent to Nogent-sur-Seine, about 160 miles from Paris, and the family moved again. The education of Camille, Louise and Paul was put into the hands of a tutor, M. Colin, whom Paul was to praise all his life for inculcating in him the precepts of Latin, spelling and math.[*] Camille's formal education seems to have ended there. On the other hand, she was an avid reader; she loved the classics and in particular the works of the poet Ossian. Louis-Prosper's library was well stocked, including almost all the classics, so that for her time, Camille was able to assimilate an amazing amount of culture, if the more by reason of her craving made acute by her adolescence and isolation.

Camille's religious education was superficial. She received the usual sacraments up until her First Communion, to which her free-thinking father remained quite indifferent. Her mother did not express either wish or opinion on the subject and remained equally indifferent. Only much later, and under the influence of Paul, did Louise Claudel rediscover her faith. Very early, Camille discovered Renan and adopted a solid agnosticism.

It is easy to imagine that in the Claudel household, like all households of that period, the subject of sexuality was taboo—an important fact to remember in order to accurately gauge Camille Claudel's artistic audacity.

During this period, Camille's creativity was already a fact. Although lost to us today, three works from that period—*Bismarck*[†], *Napoleon I* and *David and Goliath*—were significant enough, even then, for Mathias Morhardt to comment on them in his article on Camille Claudel in the *Mercure de France*. He points especially to the incontestably noble stature of her David. Camille was fifteen.

The sculptor Alfred Boucher,[‡] who was living in Nogent-sur-Seine at the time, was struck to see a child with such a promising talent. Their meeting was a major turning point in Camille's career. How or what he taught her is hard to say, for no testimony survives. Paul Claudel, who witnessed his sister's artistic formation, rarely speaks of it. As a matter of fact, the poet remains quite silent on the Nogent-sur-Seine period; more

[*] Paul Claudel, *Mémoires improvisés*, page 19.
[†] A clay bust recently discovered in Massy-sur-Blaise has a good chance of being the missing *Bismarck*.
[‡] Further information about Boucher is found on pages 166–168.

will be said later about Boucher's influence on Camille's work. During that time, Boucher introduced Camille to another sculptor, Paul Dubois.

After four years in Wassy-sur-Blaise (near Bar-le-Duc), Louis-Prosper was again transferred, this time to Rambouillet. He left his family, establishing them in Paris in April 1881 so that his children could receive the first-class education which had always been his dream. Later, Paul wrote that it was the imperious Camille who forced the family to move to Paris. He describes the event in his *Mémoires improvisés* thus: ". . . I went to a little school in Wassy—where we were six or seven [pupils]—of which I have a happy memory. And then the cataclysm in the family occurred. My sister, thinking she had the vocation of a great artist (which was unfortunately true) and having discovered clay, had started to make little statues which Alfred Boucher happened to admire, so, my sister, who was terribly determined, managed to drag the whole family to Paris—she, who wanted to sculpt, I, who, it appears, had the vocation as a writer, my other sister as a musician. . . . Finally and in short, the family was separated in two: my father stayed in Wassy while we went to Paris, to Boulevard Montparnasse, where we settled."

In Paris, Camille attended the Colarossi Academy (now the Grande Chaumière). She also rented her first studio on rue Notre-Dame-des-Champs, which she shared with three English girls—students she probably met at the academy. One of them, Jessie Lipscomb, was to remain Camille's close friend for life. Camille paid Jessie (later Mrs. Elborne) several visits in London, and the young Englishwoman, who had also become a student and friend of Rodin, was to play the difficult role of confidante in the tempestuous affair of the couple. Jessie was one of the few who never abandoned Camille. Records show that she paid Camille at least one visit at the asylum in 1924 and perhaps another in 1930. The two artists showed together in Nottingham in 1886, and the following year Jessie exhibited a portrait of Camille in terra cotta.

From time to time, Alfred Boucher dropped by the studio to give his advice to the two pretty young women. Confident in the future of his protégée, he took Camille to visit his master, Paul Dubois, the director of the Ecole des Beaux-Arts. Nothing could have been stranger to the artistic tenets of the illustrious sculptor Boucher—his smooth workmanship and his traditional values—than the improvisation and lively technique of Camille's work. At the same time, Dubois must have been struck by the originality of her little groups and his comment (quoted by Morhardt) was fairly unexpected: "Have you taken lessons with Monsieur Rodin?" he asked Camille.[*] Coming as it did from him, it is uncertain whether the comparison to a sculptor who was as yet little known—or better known by the jeers rather than the admiration of his confrères—was a compliment. Still, one can argue in response that Paul Dubois—once again guided by Alfred Boucher, a great discoverer of talent—was among those who defended Rodin against the charge of casting from a live model during the *surmoulage* scandal. In any event, Camille had never heard of Rodin, which, not so surprisingly, may go to show that one never really learns anything from anyone but oneself.

It has been suggested that Paul Dubois was one of Camille's teachers but that is not what Mathias Morhardt makes us understand. He refers to only a single meeting between the two artists and it has never been established whether Camille saw or studied with Dubois on a regular basis. What is left, directly or indirectly, thanks to Alfred Boucher, is the determining influence of the Florentine School on Camille's art. More than anything else, this kept her immune to Rodin's spell.

The first works of Camille Claudel that still exist for us today date from those formative years: *Paul Claudel at Thirteen Years of Age* (*Jeune romain*), 1881, and *Old Helen* (*La Vieille Hélène*), 1882. Far from being the experiments of a beginner, these works could easily figure in a retrospective— not as mere documentation—and confirm the already amazing mastery and precocity of the artist at the age of seventeen and eighteen.

In 1881, Alfred Boucher received the Prix du Salon and went to Italy. He asked Rodin to replace him on his visits to the studio on rue Notre-Dame-des-Champs. He particularly recommended Camille Claudel. Thus, Camille became Rodin's first female pupil. At the time, Rodin was forty and much discussed, but not yet the world-famous master.

[*] M. Morhardt, "Mlle. Camille Claudel," page 712.

Chapter 2

With Rodin (1883-1893)

Rodin crossed paths with the being who appeared destined to be his by a thousand similarities: a pity for him that he did not meet up sooner with the one meant to be his companion and disciple. She was young, charming, well-bred. . . .

Judith Cladel, *Rodin*

amille Claudel and Auguste Rodin probably met in 1883. At the time, Rodin was working in a studio at 182 rue de l'Université and Camille soon left hers on rue Notre-Dame-des-Champs to become an habitué of Rodin's. With the growing number of commissions, Rodin had begun to hire more workmen and students. However, with the exception of Jules Desbois, who, ten years Rodin's junior, was more or less his associate ever since they had worked together at the Sèvres factory, none of these students, prior to Camille, ever achieved a status higher than ordinary draftsman. In terms of creativity, of all of Rodin's disciples—who included Schnegg, Pompon and Bourdelle—Camille was the very first. Mathias Morhardt, the inexhaustible source for that period, paints us a picture of Camille totally absorbed by her work in Rodin's studio: "the silent and diligent young woman, who far from being idle, molds and sculpts the clay."[*]

[*] M. Morhardt, "Mlle. Camille Claudel," page 718.

Camille the student rapidly became Camille the collaborator. Rodin was completely absorbed in the conception and execution of *The Gates of Hell* (*La Porte d'enfer*) and Camille was doubly involved in the project—she posed and composed. She lent her body to more than one damned soul and many of the figures may have been made by her. In any case, Morhardt claims that Rodin allowed Camille to model the hands and feet of several of his larger compositions,[*] which, considering the importance Rodin attached to hands, was a great tribute to Camille.

Camille lived at home until 1888. Her parents were probably quite oblivious to the fact that their daughter's private life did not conform to the canons of behavior for a young woman of good family. Much later, Louise Claudel was to express her shock and disapproval in an undated letter to her daughter:

> How terribly he [Louis-Prosper] suffered, too, when he learned the truth about your relations with Rodin and the disgraceful comedy you performed for us. And I, I was naïve enough to invite the "Great Man" to Villeneuve with Mme. Rodin, his concubine. While you, you played the sweet innocent and were living with him as a kept woman!

Rose Beuret, Rodin's lifelong companion, was no doubt also equally oblivious to the circumstances.[†]

Love did not cramp the lovers. On the contrary, it nurtured them and Rodin's style grew more lyrical. This new cycle included works such as *The Eternal Idol* (*L'Éternelle idole*); *The Danaïd* (*La Danaïe*), for which Camille was the model; *The Sirens* (*Les Sirènes*); and *The Kiss* (*Le Baiser*)— a more externalized version of Camille's *Çacountala*. *Thought* (*La Pensée*), *Aurora* (*L'Aurore*), *St. Georges* or quite simply his *Portraits* show the extent to which Rodin was haunted not only by Camille's body but also by her face.

---

[*] M. Morhardt, "Mlle. Camille Claudel," page 712, and Judith Cladel, *Rodin, sa vie glorieuse et inconnue* (Paris: Grasset, 1936), page 226.
† Rose was Rodin's common-law wife and legally married him in the last year of his life.

Camille during this period quite suddenly affirmed and fixed her own style. The bust of Paul Claudel at sixteen dates from 1884, the time of her arrival at Rodin's studio, and is proof that her apprenticeship was over when she met the one reputed to be her master. She was twenty years old then, and the bust of Paul is a finished work that today figures in many museums as a perfect example of the sculpture of the period. The work is also a testimony to Camille's unusual precocity, comparable to that of her brother, who wrote *Tête d'or* when he was twenty.

Among Camille's existing works of that period are *Louise Claudel,* a bust of her sister, 1885; *Ferdinand de Massary,* her brother-in-law, 1888; and *Çacountala,* 1888. Of the works she exhibited at the Salon des Artistes Français, only *Çacountala* received an honorable mention, which appears very unjust to us today in view of the fact that numerous second prizes were awarded to the likes of Henri Levasseur, Eugène Quinton, Camille Lefèvre, Joseph Louis Enderlin and Antoine Gardet—names now lost in oblivion.

Late in 1888, Rodin rented yet another studio to add to his other studios. La Folie Neubourg, 68 Boulevard d'Italie, was a sumptuous, classically styled building surrounded by a wild, unkempt garden. It had once served to shelter the love of George Sand and Alfred de Musset. Whether Rodin found La Folie Neubourg before or after Camille had moved to No. 113 on the same boulevard is not clear, but in any case, he installed his young assistant in a setting that could have been idyllic had it not been half in ruins. Regardless, Rodin, for the rest of his life, would cherish happy memories of La Folie Neubourg.

It is difficult to guess whether Camille Claudel acquired enough personal autonomy at this point to leave her family and to live on the Boulevard d'Italie—one foot in La Folie, the other in her own quarters—to know, in other words, whether her independence dates from this time. No document or letter exists on the subject. And what about money? No doubt Rodin, whose own situation had vastly improved, looked after Camille's needs and paid her for her work. By then, Camille had all the qualifications of a first-class sculptor. Clay modeling held no more mysteries for her; she mixed plaster like nobody else, and she could cut marble with a force and precision that even the master Rodin never managed to equal. It would be a mistake to imagine Camille at this stage as a recluse who lived only for her master and mentor's approval rather than for her own satisfaction and love of her work.

In the meantime, Rodin was becoming famous through his large commissions, including the monument to Claude Lorrain in Nancy (1884) and *The Burghers of Calais* (*Les Bourgeois de Calais*), 1887; his highly publicized exhibitions, including the one with Monet (1889); and his participation in the Exposition Universelle (also in 1889), which unleashed a storm of protest. Rodin's position in the republican and liberal political circles of the day was also growing. (The letter he wrote the Minister of Foreign Affairs to intervene on behalf of Camille's young brother—a candidate for the Foreign Service exam—at the beginning of 1890 is a rather barbed example.) Awards, including the Legion of Honor, and receptions were the visible signs of the henceforth semi-official status of the master. Camille Claudel accompanied Rodin into that limelight while he, no doubt, must have much preferred her beautiful and lively presence to that of poor Rose Beuret, whom he hid. Together, they could be seen at the Goncourts', the Daudets' and with Octave Mirbeau, and Camille did not pass unobserved: "Tonight, at the Daudets', the little Claudel, Rodin's pupil, wearing a *canezou* embroidered with large Japanese flowers, with her childish face, her beautiful eyes, her witty sayings in that heavy country accent. . . ."[*] Important critics noticed her, too, in particular Mathias Morhardt, the editor of the newspaper *Le Temps*. As it turned out, he would be of great help to Camille.

Except for Léon Lhermitte, whose son she painted in 1889 and whose bust she did in 1894, no trace is left of the painters and sculptors Camille might have known. Her contact with the Impressionists is reduced to a single prophetic anecdote—during a trip Camille took with Rodin to visit Renoir in Cannes, she is said to have opened a shutter in order to free some birds.[†] She must have met Monet when he exhibited with Rodin at the Georges Petit gallery in 1889.

[*] E. and J. de Goncourt, *Journal. Mémoires de la vie littéraire et artistique* (Paris: Flammorion, 1959). (Entry dated May 8, 1894.)
[†] V. Frisch and J. Schipley, *Auguste Rodin: A Biography* (Frederick A. Stokes and Co., 1939), page 154.

This apparent lack of contact with contemporaries may explain Camille's isolation later and may account for the fact that, although extraordinarily talented, Camille was the mistress of an established sculptor much older than herself whose presence deprived her of the company of her artistic peers who could have become her friends as well. She was not much older than Matisse, Rouault and Bonnard, who were raised on Gauguin and Van Gogh while Camille, thanks to Rodin, was still basking in the light of Carrier-Belleuse or under the weak sunshine of Puvis de Chavannes and Eugène Carrière. Probably, too, her literary tastes inclined toward Huysmans and Renan rather than toward Rimbaud and Mallarmé. (In that respect, her brother, Paul, was more modern. In 1886, he discovered Rimbaud and in 1887 he sent Mallarmé two of his poems, which so impressed Mallarmé that he invited Paul to join his literary circle.[†]) But Camille did develop a taste for Oriental art. She was exposed to it for the first time in 1883 at the famous Japanese retrospective held at the Georges Petit gallery. Like many Parisian artists of that period, she was to become a great devotee of Japanese art, which, once she was free of Rodin, would manifest itself as a purifying influence on her own work.

A trip to the Isle of Wight with Paul in 1886 was the inspiration for an article that Camille signed "Pierre Servan." Originally, it seems, she wanted to use the name "Pierre Servau," a homonym of Cerveaux, her mother's maiden name. The piece was published in the *Revue illustrée* in August 1889, and the drawings Camille brought back from the same trip were published in the review *Art* in 1887.

The year 1887 also marks the date of Camille and Rodin's first trip to Touraine. In Azay-le-Rideau they had discovered the Château d'Islette, a refuge for their summer passion. These trips were to occur frequently, with Rodin joining Camille at the magnificent house whose owner, Madame Courcelles, took in paying guests. After 1892, the excuse Rodin gave for going there was that he was looking for features akin to those of Balzac on which to model his statue of the writer.

One letter from Camille to Rodin survives from that period:

[*] Louis Chaigne, *La Vie de Paul Claudel,* page 43. The two poems are *Le Sombre mai* and *Chanson d'automne.*

Since I have nothing else to do, I'm writing to you again. You can't imagine how pretty it is here at L'Islette.

Today, I ate in the middle room (the one used as a conservatory from where one can see both sides of the garden).

Madame Courcelles suggested (without my mentioning it at all) that if you liked, you could eat there from time to time or indeed all the time (I think it would please her). And it's so lovely here!

I went for a walk in the park. Everything has been mowed, the hay, wheat, oats, you can go all around, it's charming. If you are good enough to keep your promise, we shall be in paradise.

You can have the room you want to work in. The old lady will be at your feet, I believe.

She told me I could bathe in the river, where her daughter and the maid bathe without the slightest danger.

With your permission, I'll do the same, with great pleasure, and it will spare me the trouble of going to the hot baths in Azay. Will you be so good as to buy me a little bathing costume—dark blue with white piping, two pieces, blouse and pants (medium size), at the Louvre or Bon Marché (in serge) or at Tours.

I go to bed naked to make myself believe that you are there but when I wake up it's not the same thing.

Above all, don't deceive me anymore. [*]

These outings ended in 1894 and the next question they pose is, Did Camille have any children by Rodin? Did she go to Touraine to hide her pregnancies? Were her children placed in the hands of a nurse? The available documents supply none of the answers. Judith Cladel, Rodin's biographer, broached the subject directly to Rodin. His answer to her question, however, does not provide much of a clue:

> "Is it true that you had four children with Camille Claudel, and what became of them?"
>
> "In that case," Rodin answered, "my duty would have been simple." [†]

According to other rumors, there were two boys. Jacques Madaule inferred from Romain Rolland's correspondence that abortion had occurred. Until the truth can be firmly established, the question of children must be at

[*] June 25, 1892. Archives of the Musée Rodin.
[†] Judith Cladel, *Rodin, sa vie glorieuse et inconnue*, 1936, page 228.

13

least viewed as an added wound in poor Camille's side.

A note of caution should be added, especially to Rodin's biographers, who tend to depict those times simply as joyous escapades away from Rose Beuret. One of Rodin's letters to Rose would make it appear so:

> Don't be impatient, stay at Vivier a little longer, my studies here absorb me more and more. I feel myself reliving earlier epochs for surely I possess the atavism of these past times and looking at this architecture seems to reawake in the back of my brain things I once knew.
>
> I am turning into an architect and I must. Thus I will complete what is still missing for my *Gates*. Write to me care of general delivery in Saumur, Maine-et-Loire.
>
> I send you a kiss and ask that you take advantage of the country air to build up your strength for when you were so cold last winter.[*]

Furthermore, Rodin's *The Convalescent* (*La Convalescente*) and *The Adieu* (*L'Adieu*), both dated 1892, are indicative of painful times. Camille, whose creative genius could not be suppressed, finished *The Little Chatelaine* (*La Petite châtelaine*), also known as *Jeanne as a Child, The Inspired One,* by 1894, and the look of bewilderment on that wonderful child's face suggests that it was inspired by a mother's anguish.

By 1892, the couple's relationship had begun to deteriorate for several reasons. Probably Camille was resentful and she felt used by the opportunistic Rodin. Her maternal instincts had been cruelly thwarted, and Rose Beuret, who felt her own position menaced, was becoming more and more aggressive toward Camille. More germane, perhaps, was the conflict between two exceptional artists whose very different and yet very strong temperaments were bound to collide hurtfully in time. In view of all this, it is in fact astonishing that the liaison between Camille and Rodin managed to survive for as long as it did—fifteen years.

What more can be said about the couple, Camille Claudel and Rodin, that is not based on conjecture and fantasy but on a few personal existing documents?

[*] R. Descharnes and J.-F. Chabrun, *Auguste Rodin* (Paris: Bibliothèque des Arts, 1967), page 156.

To begin with, there is no proof that Camille was ever passionately in love with Rodin. Her letters show none of the signs usual to that state. On the contrary, there is evidence that, despite her fiery personality, Camille's affection for Rodin was tempered and quite rational—almost calculating insofar as her own ambitions were concerned.

Material and social conditions of the time did not lend themselves to excesses of passion. Camille was living partly at home and was accountable to her parents. It was unthinkable for a young girl of the bourgeoisie to be the mistress of an attached forty-year-old man, and the result would have been disastrous. Judging by the letters Louise Claudel wrote to her daughter later, Camille was capable of disguising her dissolute ways with cunning hypocrisy. Didn't she escort Monsieur and Madame—alias Rose Beuret—Rodin to Villeneuve to her own parents' home? And Rose, too, was completely unaware of the passionate love affair between the master and his pupil.

While it was true that Rodin took Camille to the best salons animated by the talk of the freethinkers of the day, the nature of the couple's relationship was never alluded to and thus, perhaps, approved of and encouraged. This suggests another side of Camille's chameleon-like nature that does not necessarily correspond to previous assumptions.

Second, the relationship between Camille and Rodin lacked the candor and equality that promote deep and lasting affection. Camille referred to Rodin as "Monsieur Rodin," while he always called his young mistress "Mademoiselle Claudel," a sign of a caste barrier. They never really lived together; their illicit escapades appeared to be satisfaction enough. The few extant letters Camille wrote to her lover have a more flirtatious than affectionate ring. She sends him precise instructions to buy a bathing suit at the Bon Marché—a typical female ploy to humiliate him. The idea of this bearded, potbellied man sent off to bargain for what was then considered an intimate piece of apparel was a big joke. When she wrote him that she slept naked so as to be that much closer to him when he was far away, she sounds more like a silly shopgirl than a woman deeply in love. Camille was never blinded by passion. Even prior to their breakup, she was aware of Rodin's weaknesses, and the drawings she did of him were not especially flattering.

Rodin, on the other hand, seems to have had a particularly strong emotional attachment to his pupil. His correspondence with Jessie Lipscomb-Elborne is very revealing, albeit difficult to make use of; many of the letters are undated, while others have either been lost or contain numerous illegible passages. The letters show Rodin worried about Camille's state of mind as well as frustrated as to how to manipulate this odd and whimsical child. He refers to Camille as "our dear stubborn one who leads us by the nose." The following letter to Jessie Lipscomb-Elborne reveals just how anxious Rodin was about his loved one:

My dear friend [he writes in 1886], I hardly know how to show my gratitude for your kindness. You have no idea how much good you do me and my poor tired spirit needs encouragement. Ah! At the moment, I'm traveling through a very ugly landscape indeed and I only can be truly happy alone and with my fantasies. Sweet nature, the sweet reality of this land bathed in pure sunshine, this beautiful France, my dear English lady, means nothing at all to me. All my strength lies over in that corner, it is there dashed and trembling and will it survive? I don't know. Send me your photographs [illegible word]. I commend both yourself and Mlle. Claudel to your gracious kindness that you may be together and remain your gracious selves.
    You have not given me anything that I've asked!
    I look inside my mailbox often, sometimes I return unexpectedly from afar, from the country, from everywhere, thinking about my letters from England.
    Don't let me languish thus in [illegible word] too much, and ask your friend to be not so lazy.
    I'm afraid I'll appear pedantic sending you the newspapers but it wasn't for mere vanity's sake, I thought to gain a bit more of your esteem and friendship. Perhaps the contrary will happen and what seemed right will be laughed at; I am certain that with [illegible word] girls have a peculiar way of undermining success and making it look ridiculous, moreover, they are right.*

The awkwardness of the style, the repetitions suggest Rodin's confusion. Contrary to the norm, Rodin's passion, too, seemed to wax rather than to wane, and the young student on whom he had thought merely to exercise

* Archives of the Musée Rodin.

16

his seigneurial rights (*droit de cuissage*)—as he did on his models—little by little dominated his thoughts.

Everything—testimonies, correspondence and, above all, the work produced during that period—leads us to believe that Rodin and Camille's first years together were joyful if not entirely happy. And however fragile the liaison, Rodin's sculptures are mute testimony to his sincere affection and growing attachment to Camille during this period.

Creatively, Rodin and Camille had established a sort of division of labor or a shared reciprocity which, much later, was to become the source of litigation. A lot of Rodin's work must have passed between Camille's hands in much the same way as did the great composite works of the past which so baffle art historians—how many Peruginos did Raphael paint? How many Rubens, Van Dyck? And notwithstanding that for a period Rodin's and Camille's styles were very similar, an expert on Camille Claudel will still be able to recognize *her* arm or *her* torso in *The Gates of Hell*. With this in mind, two of Camille's works are particularly worth mentioning: *Young Woman with a Sheaf* (*Jeune fille à la gerbe*) and *Study for a Head* (*Etude de tête*).

Young Woman with a Sheaf is a twin sister of Rodin's *Galatée*, a major work that, like *The Brother and Sister* (*Le Frère et la soeur*), underwent several metamorphoses. Yet the simple, semi-naturalistic style of this young girl is pure Camille Claudel, and the work shows none of the tensions characteristic of Rodin. Also, Rodin did not sculpt in marble, while we know that Camille excelled in that practice. Who then could be both the inspiration and the creator of *Galathea* (*Galatée*) if not Camille herself? Camille's *Study for a Head*, which has all the spontaneity of a rough draft, would later be developed and brought to life in Rodin's group *Avarice and Lewdness* (*L'Avarice et la luxure*) and once more illustrates how much the master made use of his pupil. Again, in *The Gates of Hell*, one of the heads (the study for which is called *Le Cri* and is in the Musée Rodin) must have sprung straight out of Camille's hands since it is identical to her *The Beseecher* (*L'Implorante*).

If only Rodin and Camille had been able to share their lives as well as their artistry, the latent drama could surely have been avoided. Paradoxically, their temperaments were too different, at odds and a jeopardy to their creativity. But meanwhile, Rodin was unhappier without Camille than with her. Those who knew him at the time were witnesses to the anguish he suffered over the separation, an anguish that lasted until his death. Paul Morand recounts a visit Rodin paid to his father's house in 1898: "I was very young when, one morning, Rodin appeared at our house for lunch. 'He comes all this way to try and escape the one who adores him,' my father said. The idea that a big giant of a man like Rodin could be frightened of a woman amused me. My father corrected me. 'It's not funny,' he said, 'it's a very sad story. That girl is the best pupil he ever had; she is a genius, she is very beautiful and she loves him but she's mad. Her name is Camille Claudel.' That's how I heard her name for the first time."[*] Wasn't it also true that on his deathbed Rodin asked to see his "wife," and when Rose Beuret (whom he had just married) was shown in, he murmured as if in a dream, "No, not her, the other one, the one in Paris."?[†]

The vagaries of the heart never quite provide a sufficient or ultimate explanation. It can also be supposed that Rodin sensed the disastrous psychological direction toward which Camille was headed, and his actions may have been based in the interest of his self-preservation. Be that as it may, Rodin's love for Camille was not entirely selfish. He did a great deal for her, and had Camille been less confused about her goals, Rodin would have given her the chance to establish her reputation in Paris. Thanks to him, Camille met and was liked by many of the best critics of the day: Gustave Geffroy, Octave Mirbeau, Mathias Morhardt, Roger Marx. A letter Rodin wrote to Octave Mirbeau shows his continued interest in everything pertaining to Camille even after their separation:

> For Mademoiselle Claudel who has the finest talent of the [Salon] Champ de Mars she is virtually unappreciated. You have a project for her, you've let it be known despite the times filled with lies, you have sacrificed yourself for her, for me, for your convictions. It's your heart, Mirbeau, which is the obstacle, it's your generosity that stands in your way.
>
> I don't know whether Mademoiselle Claudel will accept to go to your house on the same day as I; it is now two years since we've seen

[*] Paul Morand, *Mon plaisir . . . en littérature* (Paris: Gallimard, 1980), page 218.
[†] Judith Cladel, *Rodin*, pages 353–354.

each other and since I wrote her. I am therefore not in a position to let her know, it all depends on you. If I am to be there, Mademoiselle Claudel will have to decide.

Chavannes is going to write a letter to the minister which some friends will sign, but for the moment, I don't have much faith in it. Everyone seems to believe that Mlle. Claudel is still my protégée while, in fact, she is a misunderstood artist and well may she boast that she was up against my friends, the sculptors, and the others as well who always hindered me at the ministry for there no one knows a thing, but let us not get discouraged dear friend for I am sure of her success in the end although that poor artist will be sad, sadder still, knowing how life is, regretting and weeping, perhaps having arrived too late, a victim of her pride as an artist who works honestly, regretting the loss of her strength in this battle and for this glory come too late that brings in its place illness. . . . My letter is too discouraged, may it not fall under the eyes of Mlle. Claudel.*

Camille was received at the Daudets', the Ménard-Dorians' and at Robert Godet's. Rodin supported Camille—more so than he did any of his other students—for La Société Nationale des Beaux-Arts. He also wrote countless letters to newspapers; the following one to the editor of *Le Courrier de l'Aisne* is an example of Rodin's efforts on Camille's behalf:

Since you were good enough to mention my name among the sculptors at the [Salon] *Champ de Mars,* allow me to point out to you my pupil, Mlle. Camille Claudel, who comes from the department and who, at this very moment, has achieved a great success with my bust located in the place of honor at the exhibition. Lhermitte, an artist emeritus also from the department, has just commissioned a bust from her as well. My pupil has already done a bust of one of his children. The Parisian papers have created a reputation for her. I would personally be flattered if you could include the already well known name of Mlle. Camille Claudel in your newspaper. *L'Art français,* in the issue on the *Champ de Mars,* devoted a very large photograph to her.

Be assured, sir, while I ask to be forgiven for my initiative and my request, etc. . . . May 19, 1892.†

Although Rodin was never to marry Camille, Camille probably believed in the possibility of their union and wished for it as a means of salvaging

---

* Cited in Paul Claudel, *Journal 2* (Paris: Gallimard, 1969), pages 626–627.
† This letter is reproduced with the kind permission of Monsieur Alphandéry.

years of compromise, unfinished business and accumulated bitterness. At the turn of the century—so close to us in years yet so far in spirit—a woman who was both single and an artist was a living scandal, and in the eyes of society Camille had no other choice but to marry the great artist or expiate her sins in a nunnery. Nor could she avoid hearing the voices, raised like a Greek chorus, especially those of the Claudel women, her mother and her sister, a constant harangue designed to drive even a less fragile person mad. Camille's failure was much more than an emotional defeat. It represented a professional failure that filled her with feelings of powerlessness and worthlessness—later, no doubt, the cause of her unhappiness and self-destructive tendencies.

As of 1893, Camille lived and worked at 113 Boulevard d'Italie, thus separating both her work and her daily life from Rodin's. Nevertheless, she continued to see him, to go with him on holidays, to ask him for his advice, as an undated letter she wrote him shows:

> Here's a letter I've begun to Monsieur Gauchez which I've made a mess of, as you can see and which is certainly stupid. Could you correct it for me please and put in a *belle tartine* [overblown phrase] on movement and the search for nature etc. I can't possibly manage it on my own.[*]

In 1895, Camille wrote to congratulate Rodin on his *Balzac*.

> You told Le Bossé to ask me to write you my opinion of your statue of Balzac: I find it very beautiful and the best of all your studies on the subject. Especially, the very accentuated effect of the head which contrasts with the simplicity of the drapery, it is absolutely right and very impressive. I also like the idea of the empty sleeves which are very expressive of that man's negligent spirit. . . .[†]

Afterwards, there is nothing more between them.

The meeting between Camille and Debussy took place between 1888 and 1889, before her break with Rodin. The nature of their relationship has been the source of much conjecture among biographers—was it merely

[*] Archives of the Musée Rodin.
[†] Ibid.

a friendship or a passionate liaison? Chances are it was a brief one-sided infatuation: Debussy may have fallen in love with Camille while she was still too preoccupied with Rodin. Debussy had just returned to Paris from Rome. He was living with Gabrielle Dupont, a beautiful green-eyed woman who was his companion for many years. Not yet thirty years old, Debussy was still an unknown musician. He was said to hate Rodin's work, describing it as "gamey romanticism" (*au romantisme faisandé*). Debussy himself was working on *La Demoiselle élue* at the time. Robert Godet, who regularly invited both Camille and Debussy to his house, confirmed the bond that existed between the two artists by describing Camille as sitting rapt and silent while Debussy played the piano. We also know that Camille introduced Debussy to Japanese art.[*]

In 1891, Camille and Debussy suddenly stopped seeing each other. The reasons remain mysterious yet Debussy's feelings were clearly expressed in a letter he wrote to Robert Godet on February 13, 1891:

> . . . the predictable and sad end of this episode I told you about; a banal ending with anecdotes, words that never should have been spoken. I noticed this strange transposition, at the moment I heard those harsh words fall from her lips, I heard inside me those uniquely adorable ones she had once said! And the false notes (alas real!) clashed with those singing within me, tearing me apart, without my hardly being able to understand. . . .
>
> Ah! I really loved her and with all the more sad ardor by the evident signs I felt that never would she take certain steps to engage her whole spirit and that she was keeping herself inviolable against queries to her heart's solidity. Now, it remains to be seen whether she was what I was looking for! If it wasn't all emptiness!
>
> Despite it all, I weep for the disappearance of the Dream of this Dream.[†]

Probably nothing summarizes so well the relationship of the two young artists than the last words of Debussy's letter. Always and until his death, Debussy kept Camille's *The Waltz* (*La Valse*) on top of the mantelpiece

---

[*] Edward Lockspeiser, *Claude Debussy* (Paris: Fayard, 1980), page 284.
[†] Claude Debussy, *Lettres à deux amis;* preface by Robert Godet (Paris: José Corti, 1942).

of his studio (without its ever being established where he got it). Jealousy—of Debussy or Rodin—has been the suggested cause of Rodin and Camille's separation[*] but again, lack of documents relegates this explanation to the realm of conjecture.

Camille and Debussy's relationship, however, does allow for one question: What role in Camille's life and work did music play? Jules Renard describes Camille as tone deaf and quite pleased to be so:

> At the Claudels', dinner and a strange evening. His sister said to me: You frighten me, Monsieur Renard, you will make fun of me in one of your books. Her powdered face was animated only by her eyes and mouth. Sometimes, it looked dead. She hated music, she says it out loud just how she thinks it while her brother rages, his nose in his plate, and one can feel his hands clenching in anger and his legs trembling underneath the table.[**]

Yet many of Camille Claudel's works have a musical theme—*The Waltz* (*La Valse*), *The Flute Player* (*La Joueuse de flûte*), *The Blind Singer* (*Aveugle chantant*), to name a few—and her musical tastes probably ran counter to those of Rodin. Rodin hated Wagner and said that *Parsifal* was just a bad Mass; as for Debussy, Rodin said he never understood anything he wrote, and besides, it bored him. Camille, on the other hand, declared herself a supporter of Moussorgsky; in a letter to Mathias Morhardt, she apologizes for not being able to attend one of the composer's concerts.[†]

On this note, a phase of Camille's life came to a close—her youthful romances—and from this point on, there would be no more serious romantic attachments. As for her youth, she was to describe it herself much later in a letter to her dealer, Eugène Blot: "A novel . . . an epic even, an *Iliad* or an *Odyssey*. It would require a Homer to tell it. I won't attempt to do so today and I don't want to sadden you. I have fallen into a void. I live in a world that is so curious, so strange. Of the dream that was my life, this is the nightmare."[‡]

---

[*] John Tancock, *The Sculpture of Auguste Rodin* (Philadelphia: Museum of Art, 1976), page 590, note 3.
[**] Jules Renard, *Journal* (Paris: Gallimard, 1967), page 185. (Dated March 9, 1895.)
[†] Claudel Fund, Bibliothèque Nationale.
[‡] Judith Cladel Archives, Lilly Library, Indiana University, Bloomington. (May 24, 1935.)

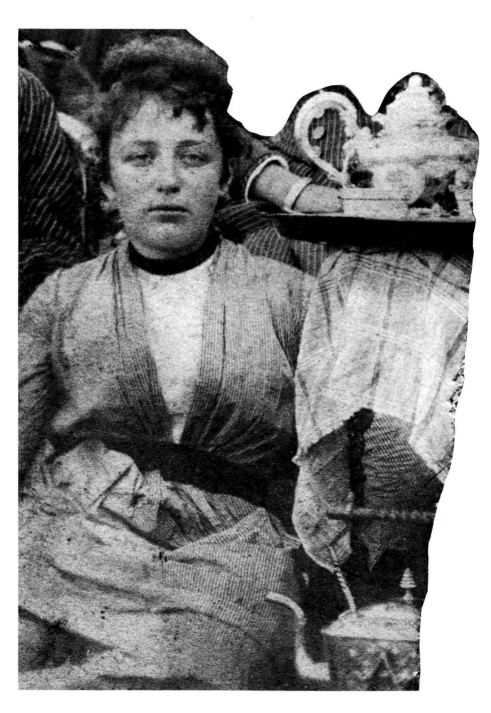

1. Camille Claudel around 1894.
(Private collection)

24

3. *The Claudel family in 1887, Boulevard de Port-Royal: in front, Louise; behind her, her mother; directly above Mme. Claudel, from left to right: Louis-Prosper Claudel, Paul, and Camille.*

4. Alfred Boucher, bust of his mother.
(Musée de Nogent-sur-Seine)

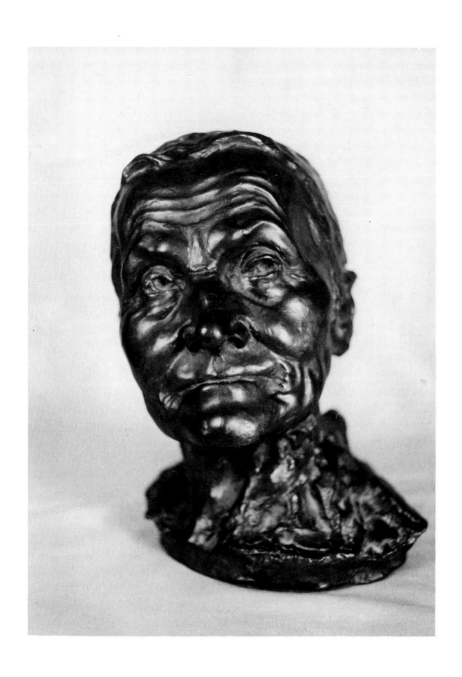

5. Old Helen. *Bronze, 1882,*
11 × 7 × 8¼ inches.

6. Young Roman.
Bronze, 1881,
15¾ × 14½ × 8½ inches.

7. Mennie Jean de Gerardmer. *Charcoal sketch, 1885,*
19¾ × 15½ inches.

29

8. *Auguste Rodin*, Thought *(for which Camille was the model)*, *1886.* (Musée Rodin)

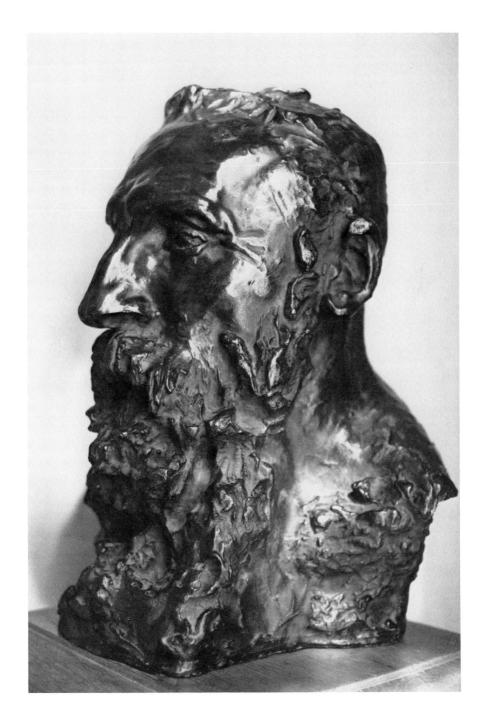

9. Bust of Rodin. Bronze, 1892,
16 × 10¼ × 11 inches.

31

10. Portrait of Maria Paillette. *Oil, 1887,
31½ × 23¼ inches.*

11. Paul Claudel. *Colored pencil, 1888,*
17 × 13¾ inches.

13. Çacountala. *Marble, 1905,*
37½ × 32¼ × 15¾ inches.

OPPOSITE: *12. Auguste Rodin,* The Eternal Idol, *1889.*
(Musée Rodin)

35

14. *Auguste Rodin*, Galatea, *around 1890.*
(Musée Rodin)

15. Young Woman with a Sheaf. *Terra cotta, around 1890,*
14¼ × 8¼ × 8¼ inches.

16.

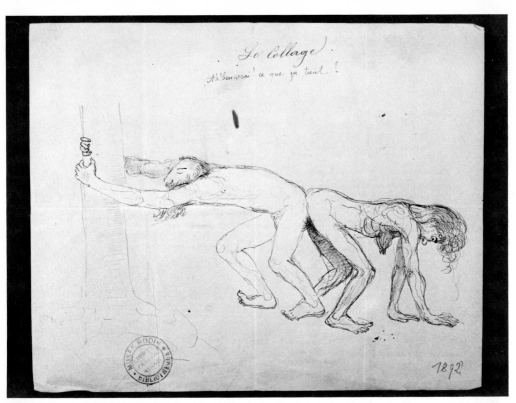

17.

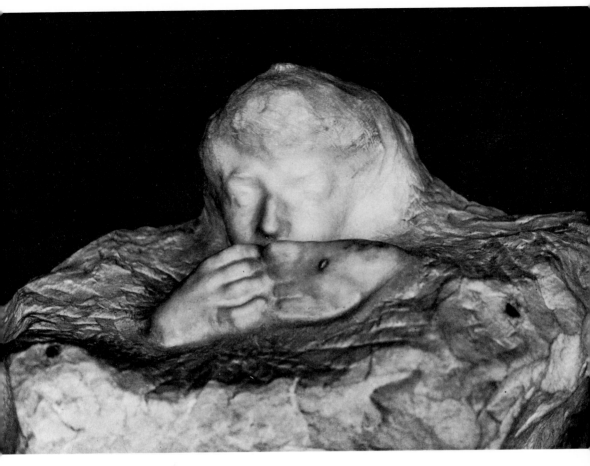

18. *Auguste Rodin*, The Adieu *(for which Camille was the model)*,
1892. (Musée Rodin)

OPPOSITE: *16. Le Collage, around 1892.* (Musée Rodin) *17.* Le
Système cellulaire, *around 1892.* (Musée Rodin)

19. Camille wears the bicorne of her brother Paul, who was appointed vice-consul to New York in 1893. The photograph probably dates from the same year.

Mon cher Paul

Ta dernière lettre m'a
fait bien rire, je te
remercie de tes floraisons
américaines mais j'en
ai reçu moi-même toute
une bibliothèque, effet
de neige, oiseaux qui
volent etc. La
bêtise anglaise est sans
bornes, il n'y a pas.
de sauvages qui fabriquent
de pareilles amulettes
je te remercie de l'offre
que tu me fais de me
prêter de l'argent : cette
fois-ci, ce n'est pas.
de refus car j'ai épuisé
les 600 f de maman
et voici l'époque de mon
terme, je te prie donc
si cela ne te cause aucun
dérangement de

m'envoyer 150 à 200f.

J'ai eu dernièrement des malheurs : un mouleur pour se venger a détruit à mon atelier plusieurs choses finies, mais je ne veux pas t'attrister.

Les Daudet doivent venir me voir la semaine prochaine avec madame Alphonse Daudet. Ils sont toujours très aimables, je ne vois plus souvent Schwob et Pottecher, Mathieu a disparu;

Je suis toujours attelé à mon groupe de trois, je vais mettre un arbre penché qui exprimera la destinée; j'ai beaucoup d'idées nouvelles qui te plairont énormément, je suis tout à fait enthousiasmé... rentrer dans

ton esprit voici un
croquis de la dernière
esquisse (la Confidence)

trois personnages en
écoutent un autre
derrière un paravent

le Bénédicité

arbre

des personnages tout
petits autour d'une grande
table écoutent la prière
avant le repas

La Dimanche

trois bonshomme en
blouse neuve et
pareille juchés sur
une très haute
charrette partent pour
la messe

La Faute.

une jeune fille accroupie
sur un banc seulement,
ses parents la regardent
tout étonnés

J'ai un grand grand
plaisir à travailler.
Je vais envoyer au
Salon de Bruxelles
le petit groupe des
amoureux, le
buste à capuchon,
la Valse en bronze
la petite de l'Islette.

Au salon prochain
le buste de Shermette
avec une draperie
qui vole
et le groupe de
trois si j'ai fini

voilà comment il sera

tout en largeur

et puis j'ai un
autre groupe dans
la tête que tu
trouveras épatant
Tu ne me parles
jamais de ce que
tu écris : as-tu de
nouveaux livres en
train ?.. -

Plusieurs de
mes amis m'ont
dit qu'ils
allaient acheter
Tête d'or
Tu ne seras pas
là pour le
vernissage,
je le regrette beaucoup
Il a fait dernièrement
un froid terrible
j'ai été obligé de
faire du feu la
nuit
Je te serre les mains

Camille

tu vois que ce n'est
plus du tout du Rodin,
et c'est habillé
je vais faire des petites
terres cuites
Dépêche toi de revenir
pour voir tout ça

le violoneux

trois petits enfants
assis par terre écoutent
un vieux joueur de
violon
qu'en dis tu ? . . . . .
c'est à toi seulement
que je confie ces trouvaille
ne les montre pas !

28. Louis-Prosper Claudel. *Pencil, around 1897,*
23¼ × 19 inches.

29. *Camille Claudel sculpting.*

OPPOSITE: *30. Camille Claudel sculpting* Perseus and the Gorgon *in her studio at 113 Boulevard d'Italie.*

31. Bust of Paul Claudel at Forty-two Years of Age. *Bronze, 1910, 19 × 21 × 7½ inches.*

32. Paul Claudel with a bust of Camille sculpted by Rodin, entitled Mademoiselle Claudel. *Bronze, 1884.*

33. Camille Claudel around 1935.

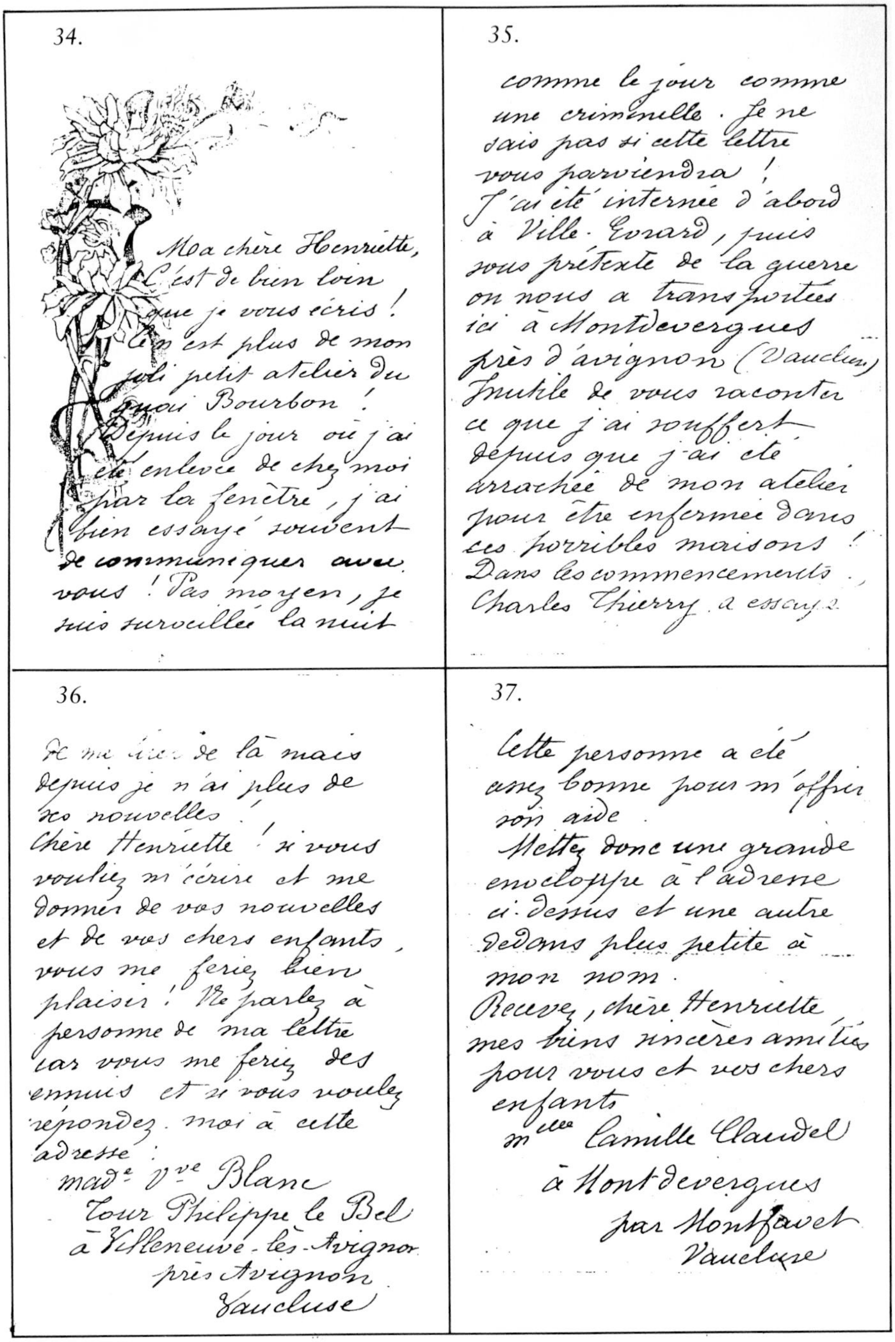

34.

Ma chère Henriette,
C'est de bien loin
que je vous écris!
Ce n'est plus de mon
joli petit atelier du
quai Bourbon!
Depuis le jour où j'ai
été enlevée de chez moi
par la fenêtre, j'ai
bien essayé souvent
de communiquer avec
vous! Pas moyen, je
suis surveillée la nuit

35.

comme le jour comme
une criminelle. Je ne
sais pas si cette lettre
vous parviendra!
J'ai été internée d'abord
à Ville-Evrard, puis
sous prétexte de la guerre
on nous a transportées
ici à Montdevergues
près d'Avignon (Vaucluse)
Inutile de vous raconter
ce que j'ai souffert.
Depuis que j'ai été
arrachée de mon atelier
pour être enfermée dans
ces horribles maisons!
Dans les commencements,
Charles Thierry a essayé

36.

de me tirer de là mais
depuis je n'ai plus de
ses nouvelles!
Chère Henriette! si vous
vouliez m'écrire et me
donner de vos nouvelles
et de vos chers enfants,
vous me feriez bien
plaisir! Ne parlez à
personne de ma lettre
car vous me feriez des
ennuis et si vous voulez
répondez-moi à cette
adresse:
madᵉ Vve Blanc
Tour Philippe le Bel
à Villeneuve-lès-Avignon
près Avignon
Vaucluse

37.

Cette personne a été
assez bonne pour m'offrir
son aide.
Mettez donc une grande
enveloppe à l'adresse
ci-dessus et une autre
dedans plus petite à
mon nom.
Recevez, chère Henriette
mes biens sincères amitiés
pour vous et vos chers
enfants.
Mᵉˡˡᵉ Camille Claudel
à Montdevergues
par Montfavet
Vaucluse

34–37. Letter from Camille Claudel to Henriette Thierry, written in the asylum at Montdevergues.

Chapter 3

The Years of Solitude and the Last of Her Art (1893-1913)

. . . I will be able to escape from my bonds only after being subjected to thousands of terrible misfortunes. Ability cannot prevail against the inevitable.

Aeschylus, *Prometheus Bound*

When Camille broke off with Rodin (he, in any case, was forced to abandon the decaying La Folie and move from Paris to Meudon), she sequestered herself in the apartment on the Boulevard d'Italie which also served as her studio. Apparently, it was such a mess that visitors were shocked and Mathias Morhardt referred to it as "the court of miracles."[*] Camille was only thirty years old then and certainly still young enough to undertake working alone. Her first works from that period, *The Waltz* and *Clotho,* are masterpieces (both were shown at the Salon of 1893) but were created under the auspices of Rodin and no longer represented what Camille wanted to do. At this point, she was determined to break with the style of Rodin's school—a courageous move since she had no other influences or sources to fall back on. For her, Rodin stood for a

[*] M. Morhardt, "Mlle. Camille Claudel," page 731.

sort of Académie and he had little contact with the Ecole des Beaux-Arts. According to Morhardt, who saw Camille frequently and who recorded their conversation together, Camille was now more interested in capturing street scenes and the ordinary outside world outside her window. Whenever she was not sculpting, she was observing passersby or spending long hours studying at the Louvre or the Musée Guimet, accumulating a large number of notes and sketches, in the manner of Daumier, based on her observations. Her studio, Morhardt wrote, was filled with figurines, a sort of repository of the mores and attitudes of the day, all of which, unfortunately, have been either lost or destroyed.

The letter Camille wrote to Paul in 1893 or 1894, which included her drawings, is full of valuable insights into Camille's work.[*] (The letter, complete with drawings, is reproduced in illustrations 20–27, pages 41–48.

My dear Paul,
Your last letter made me laugh a lot, thank you for the flowery presents from America but I've already received a whole library of them, snow effects, birds that fly, etc. The stupidity of the English knows no bounds—no savages in the world would produce such amulets. Thank you for the offer to lend me money; this time I won't refuse as I've spent the 600 francs from Maman and now my rent is due, so if it is not inconvenient, please send me 150 or 200 francs.

I've had some bad luck lately, a mouleur [caster], out of revenge, destroyed several finished pieces in my studio, but I don't want to sadden you.

The Daudets are supposed to come and see me next week with Mme. Alphonse Daudet. They are always so kind and I don't see Schwob and Pottecher often anymore, Mathïeu has disappeared.

I am still harnessed to my group of three. I'm going to put in a leaning tree which will represent destiny; I have a lot of new ideas which you will like enormously—[illegible word] absolutely enthuse you [illegible word] correspond with your ideas—here is a sketch of my latest work [The Gossipers].

(Sketch)

Three people listening to another behind a screen.

[*] Paul Claudel was vice-consul in New York and Boston at the time. The letter, is one of the few that can be dated with relative accuracy. (Camille Claudel never dated her letters.)

Saying Grace

(*Sketch*)

Some very small people sitting around a large table listening to grace before the meal.

Sunday

(*Sketch*)

Three farmers in the same new shirts on top of a big wagon on their way to Mass.

The Transgression

(*Sketch*)

A young girl huddled on a bench is crying while her parents look on in astonishment.

I get great great pleasure from working. I'm going to send to the Brussels Salon the little group of lovers, the bust with the hood, *The Waltz* in bronze, *The Little Girl from Islette!* And to the next salon, the bust of Lhermitte with a drapery that flies away and the group of three if I've finished, here is how it will be

(*Sketch*)

all in width

and then, I have another group in my head that you will like.

You never speak about what you are writing: have you got another book in progress? . . .

Several of my friends have told me that they are going to buy *Tête d'Or*. You won't be here for the opening, I'm so sorry about that . . .

It's been terribly cold lately, I've been obliged to light a fire at night.

I shake your hand,
Camille

You see it's no longer at all like Rodin and [they] are dressed. I'm going to do some terra cottas.

Hurry back to see all of this.

The Violin Player

(*Sketch*)

Three small children sitting on the ground are listening to an old violin player.

What do you think?

It is only to you that I confide these, don't show them!

Acting in accordance with what she had told Morhardt, Camille devoted her energies to trying to capture psychological overtones. She wanted to create a new genre of narrative sculpture based on everyday life. Her phrase "And [they] are dressed!" is significant. Drapery, always an important element in Camille's sculpture, became even more so. (Rodin, on the other hand, was still obsessed with nudity to the point of portraying poor old Victor Hugo as if taken by surprise in his bath.) *The Gossipers* (*Les Causeuses*), which was shown at the Salon du Champ-de-Mars in 1895, inaugurates Camille's new style and was followed by *Deep in Thought* (*La Profonde pensée*), also known as *Woman Kneeling Before a Hearth* in 1898 and the *Old Blind Singer* (*Vieil aveugle chantant*), done between 1895 and 1898. The other works of that period were either destroyed or lost.

Only *Maturity* (*L'Age mûr*), Camille's most ambitious group, which dates from 1895, shows the tenacity of Rodin's influence on Camille's art. A dramatization of her own life, the statue shows an old man with Rodin's big feet and hands being led away by an old hag while a beautiful young nude tries vainly to hold him back. Later, Paul Claudel called it "a petrified moment" in his article *"Ma Soeur Camille":* "This young nude girl is my sister! My sister Camille, imploring, humiliated, on her knees; this superb, this proud young woman had depicted herself in this fashion."

Camille also continued to do portraits: the painter *Léon Lhermitte* in 1895, *Count Christian de Maigret in the Costume of Henry II* in 1899 (*Le Comte de Maigret en costume Henri II*), *Paul Claudel at Forty-two Years of Age* (*Paul Claudel à quarante-deux ans*) in 1910, several undated *Children's Heads* (*Têtes d'enfants*), *The Alsatian Woman* (*L'Alsacienne*) in 1902, two mythological figures that were commissions and done more in accordance with the style of the times—*Hamadryad* (*L'Hamadryade*), 1897, and *Perseus and the Gorgon* (*Persée et la Gorgone*), 1898. *Fortune* (*La Fortune*) and *The Flute Player* (*The Siren*), both finished before 1905, show that Camille had attained her own form of classicism—a prelude to success that illness would cut short.

Although not negligible, the list of Camille Claudel's sculptures between 1893 and 1913 appears short, considering that it was the work of twenty years. Those who knew her then described her as a recluse, avoiding people and working relentlessly. Morhardt said that the only person Camille ever spoke to was her concierge. There were few trips—one to Guernsey in 1894, one to the Pyrenees with her brother and his friends, the Francquis and the Berthelots, in 1905—even fewer events in her life worth mentioning, no liaisons and no financial rewards. The only occurrence of note during that period was that Camille served on the jury of La Société Nationale des Beaux-Arts from 1893 to 1899.

Camille, it appears, grew fiercer each day. She had never really been social—a typical Claudel in that respect—and now she avoided nearly everyone. Friendships were rare—she had only one faithful childhood friend from Villeneuve-sur-Fère, Maria Paillete. Rodin, surrounded by glory, elegant dinners in town and more and more officially ensconced in his career, grew remote, and when he invited Camille to receptions, she refused—her excuse was that she had nothing to wear. "I can't go where you suggest," she wrote in one of her letters to Rodin, "as I have no hat or shoes, mine are all worn out."[*] And although their relationship did not actually terminate until 1898, already in 1896 Camille asked Mathias Morhardt to intervene on her behalf by telling Rodin not to come and see her anymore.

The sad truth was that Camille was languishing in semi-poverty. Her

[*] Archives of the Musée Rodin.

correspondence during those years was filled with pleas for help; she begged for money with which to pay the rent. Not so surprising, for what could a woman alone, with no one to turn to, no family fortune, do? She did manage to keep her sense of humor. In 1905, she wrote her dealer, Eugène Blot: "Apart from all that, I perhaps would not have answered your invitation to go to the Salon d'Automne; I don't want to get involved in administrative affairs, nor do I know anything about them, and furthermore, I can't appear in public in the outfits I own at this hour. I am like *Peau d'âne** or Cinderella condemned to stay by the ashes of the chimney without the hope of ever seeing the Fairy Godmother or Prince Charming arrive to turn my rags into fashionable dresses."[†]

In addition, sculpting is a costly occupation. Not only did Camille have to pay the rent and buy raw materials; her expenses included workmen and casters, a sum total of at least 1,500 to 1,800 francs a year. The price of clay, armature and casting ranged from 600 to 800 francs, models from 400 to 1,000 francs, to say nothing of a work in marble, which was even more expensive. (At the time, good Italian marble cost 1,500 to 2,000 francs per cubic meter, and a life-sized statue required two cubic meters.)[‡] No wonder Camille accumulated debts and was hounded by creditors.

At one point, she was fined 200 francs, including the accrued interest, and to pay it, she was forced to borrow money from a friend who in turn accused Camille of keeping a lover. Camille described the circumstances in a bitter letter to Eugène Blot:

> By way of anecdote, let me tell you that the friendly Adonis has once again plied me with an ill-considered complaint: we went before a referee with pasty faces, which I haven't done since I went to court for the modest sum of eighteen sous which I was unwilling to pay an honest laborer. Result: I was taken for an exploiting capitalist of the poor wretch that I had so odiously tortured. Following which, I borrowed money from one of my friends who thought it was a bad joke, accused me of having a lover whom I was paying and suggested that in the future I find a better way of going about it.

* Translator's note: *Peau d'âne* is a French fairy tale written in verse by Perrault (1715).
[†] Archives of the Musée Rodin.
[‡] Jacques Lethève, *La Vie quotidienne des artistes français au XIXᵉ siècle* (Paris: Hachette, 1968).

60

Ever since, he turns his back when he sees me arrive with my plasters. Indeed, he considers me a plague, a cholera for all those considerate and generous people who are concerned with the question of art and at the sight of me with my plasters, the king of the Sahara himself would take flight."[*]

Camille's father and brother helped her out financially throughout this period (without the knowledge of the two Louises), and it was also likely that Camille accepted commissions for such objects as lamps and ashtrays (which brought her work closer to that of Art Nouveau), but those unsigned models have never been identified. All the same, Camille's work did not pass entirely unnoticed. Nearly every year, she exhibited at the Société Nationale des Beaux-Arts, the Salon d'Automne or the Salon des Indépendants, and showed at both the Bing and Eugène Blot galleries. Camille also exhibited abroad—in Brussels at the Salon de la Libre Esthétique in 1884, in Geneva, in Rome, maybe even in New York. Her *Hamadryad,* for instance, was shown at the Exposition Universelle in 1900, an honor, to be sure, and right next to the work of Rodin, who had built an entire pavilion to house his art.

Collectors, too, were interested in Camille's art, among them, Robert Godet, the painter Léon Lhermitte, Johany Peytel, the Count and Countess of Maigret, and Maurice Fenaille, to whom she wrote: "With your help, I hope to finish *The Wave* (*La Vague*) if you would be kind enough not to withdraw your patronage to an artist who is indeed French yet not much encouraged; and who after exhibiting for fifteen years at the Salon finds herself in the same place as when she started in spite of the false promises made her by certain people."[†] Critics also paid attention to Camille. Gustave Geffroy frequently wrote about her in *La Vie artistique.* In 1897, Henry de Braisne published a flattering article on Camille in *La Revue idéaliste,* more of a portrait than a critique, and in 1898, the faithful Mathias Morhardt, editor-in-chief of *Le Temps,* published his homage to her in *Mercure de France*—a veritable poem. In 1903, in a magazine called *Fémina,* Gabrielle Reval wrote that Camille Claudel was the best French sculptor.

Perhaps the determining factor in Camille's career was the great disparity

[*] Archives of the Musée Rodin.
[†] Claudel Fund, Bibliothèque Nationale.

between public recognition and the admiration of her artistic peers. In order to succeed as a sculptor, she had to have official commissions, but despite a few tentative offers she never really received any. At a banquet, for instance, in honor of Puvis de Chavannes on January 16, 1895, the participants (all of whom were famous and included Chavannes, Rodin and Albert Besnard) decided to offer Camille's marble *Clotho* to the Luxembourg Museum to commemorate the event; not only was that a great honor for Camille but it also showed the extent of the power of old Puvis de Chavannes. Later, there was talk of asking her to do a monument to Alphonse Daudet. On January 21, 1897, Mathias Morhardt wrote a letter on Camille's behalf to Rodin:[*]

> My dear friend,
>   La Société des Gens de Lettres is doing a monument to Alphonse Daudet. It seems to me that the Daudet family will be consulted. Couldn't you send a word to Léon Daudet, to remind him of Mlle. Claudel. I'm sure he will listen to you. Also, couldn't Octave Mirbeau write a word. What a beautiful statue she would make, isn't that so? . . .

The possibility of a statue to Auguste Blancqui was also discussed, but again Camille's hopes were dashed.

Had Camille been less exacting, less hard to please and willing to lower her high standards, she might have been content to be a decorative artist. As it was, proud and mindless of social success, she was looking for new avenues in sculpture while only barely managing to subsist in semi-obscurity and poverty. As Rodin's fame and glory grew, so must have her scorn and resentment, and she began to doubt the genius she had once so admired. Nothing could have been more alien to Camille's nature than Rodin's official career, his involvement with academics and Beaux-Arts lackeys, and much worse, in view of her artistic values, was Rodin's work, which instead of following more experimental paths had become progressively commercial.

In 1896, Camille left the Boulevard d'Italie to live for a year at 63 rue de Turenne. In 1899, she moved again to the Ile-St.-Louis, to 19 Quai Bourbon.

[*] Archives of the Musée Rodin.

62

There, in a dreary, cluttered and disorderly two-room apartment, she lived until 1913. Although she was still young, slender and beautiful when Henry de Braisne paid her a visit in 1897, the photographs of Camille after 1899 show a heavy-set woman looking a lot older than her years. In spite of *The Gossipers*, Camille's career was not making much headway nor could she prove to the critics that she was no longer just a pupil of Rodin or that, from now on, her art was entirely her own. Her extreme solitude, her sense of undeserved failure, her resentment, however, do not provide enough of an explanation for the persecution complex that was to dominate the rest of Camille's life.

There are two hypotheses: Camille can be viewed as completely alienated and her growing hatred for Rodin a resulting pathological symptom, or else she can be viewed as the victim of a neurotic obsession which deforms and exaggerates the perceptions of a healthy mind. The facts as we now know them, since the medical dossiers have been made available, lead us to adopt both hypotheses at once, notwithstanding the testimony of those who actually saw Camille at the time—for example, Eugène Blot and Henry Asselin, who were both not entirely convinced that what they saw were the signs of madness. But what value is the testimony of friends who saw her only occasionally compared with that of her neighbors and the doctors? But before we examine Camille's pathology, let us look for the causes.

The persecutor who took form in her mind was never the public or the critics but Rodin, always Rodin, who could assume a thousand different dreadful shapes—her models, her workmen, her admirers, her casters, even her friends. In her delirium, all of them were part of a plot whose sole function was to rob Camille of her ideas and to plagiarize and ruin her work. A few documents, Camille's own letters, some testimony of contemporaries are the only guides we have to this tormented mind—and especially those of Paul Claudel, whose fury toward Rodin is justifiable in this respect. But the real answer may perhaps be found only by examining and studying Rodin's works.

What was this terrifying reality which led Camille to believe in a "Rodin conspiracy"? It is difficult to imagine that the great sculptor ever actually plagiarized or stole from Camille Claudel. The reality is much more complex: this obsession with theft and plagiarism was a subtle and unconscious transference—Camille had given away a part of her genius to Rodin and now she could not get it back from him. Rodin's critics agree that the style he developed in the 1880s coincides with his meeting Camille.

Camille was barely twenty years old and at what Rimbaud called "the age of genius," while Rodin was over forty, past his prime and out of touch with his creative sources. Left alone, his style might have evolved toward that of a neo-Michelangelo. Instead, all of a sudden, he was shown a new avenue. Once Camille had left, however, that avenue turned into a dead end.

This collaboration between passion and creation, between two lovers who shared the same profession, workplace and subject matter brings us to a troubling conclusion: Camille, for fifteen years, was both Rodin's muse and his hand, and Rodin's famous phrase "I showed her where to find the gold, but the gold she finds is truly hers" takes on a strange and revealing significance. The temptation is to interpret it differently: "The gold she finds belongs to me."

This symbiosis, unique in the history of art, gave birth to a mixed work. It has been said of Camille that she made some Rodins; likewise a portion of Rodin's work is said to echo Camille's. It has also been pointed out that from *Balzac* on—Rodin began it precisely in 1893—Rodin's inspiration began to falter. Most of the many works he produced between 1893 and his death very often turn out to be variations of the "damned," "bacchantes" and "couples" from *The Gates of Hell.* Until 1913, then, at exhibitions and in collectors' homes, Camille was more than likely to see larger and modified versions of her own statues—works inspired by her ideas or created thanks to them.

> Each time I put a new model into circulation, millions roll for the founders, the caster, the artists and the merchants and for me . . . zero plus zero equals zero. . . . Last year, my neighbor, M. Picard [a friend of Rodin's], the brother of a detective, broke into my apartment with a passkey. Against the wall there was a woman in yellow. Since, he's made several women in yellow, the same size exactly as mine which he has shown . . . since, they are all making women in yellow and when I will want to show mine, they will take sides against me and forbid me to. . . . Another time, a cleaning woman put a narcotic in my coffee which made me sleep for twelve solid hours. During that time, the woman

went inside my dressing room and took *The Woman with the Cross*.
Result, three figures of *Woman with the Cross*.*

This small number of statues—they can be counted on the fingers of
one hand—that Camille actually signed while she was working with Rodin
is in a way astounding. By all accounts, she worked long and hard and
not just on beginner's exercises but on works of great quality. What happened
then to all those days, months, years of sculpting unless she was creating
works for Rodin? Probably, too, it did not matter to her at the time for,
typical of a woman, she was ready to give Rodin everything—not only
her life but her art. But once his hold was broken and affection had turned
into hate, despair set in. Camille was certain that she had been robbed of
her vital energy, in a sense of her life. How else to explain that she considered
it an insult to be taken for one of Rodin's students when it was meant as
a compliment? In 1902, Camille refused an invitation to show in Prague
largely on the grounds that she did not want to see her work exhibited
next to Rodin's. "It is true," she wrote the organizer of the exhibition,
"that in Prague, if I agreed to show next to M. Rodin, he would act as he
pleased to keep me under his protection and pretend that my works were
his inspiration; that way my chances of being successful, since they come
from him, would return to him directly. But I'm not in the mood to let
myself be fooled any longer by that scoundrel and deceiver (the master of
us all, he claims)—his greatest pleasure is to make fun of everyone."†

To see the man whom she had inspired with her own talent advance
toward fame and glory while she was being swallowed up by darkness
must have been too much for Camille's proud and solitary spirit. Her reason
collapsed. From 1905 onward, her obsessions, her anguish were first fix-
ations, then psychoses. Her letters to Paul, to whom she confided everything
while begging him not to reveal her thoughts to anyone, indicated not
mere confusion but a real paranoia in need of forceful therapy. Rodin
had used her, Camille could no longer distinguish between works in progress
and those she had done with him, time contracted, and the artistic process

*Undated letter from Camille Claudel to Paul Claudel. Claudel Fund, Bibliothèque
Nationale.
†Archives of the Musée Rodin.

65

became quite deranged. Among Camille's imagined persecutors, the Huguenots were the most menacing, an allusion to the founder, Hébrardt, who had not dealt honestly with Camille. In addition, the idea that her works were being copied obsessed her. *The Gossipers* had created a sensation in the Beaux-Arts circle, and since ideas may have been rarer there than manual dexterity, Camille, no doubt, had many imitators. But plagiarism is more or less encouraging for the healthy mind while to the damaged one it becomes an outrage—more so for Camille, since she had persuaded herself that others were making fortunes off her ideas. In her mind she multiplied their profits by hundreds of thousands of francs.

Camille's difficulties and obsessions were compounded by family discord. She had become persona non grata in Villeneuve, among her own, where she should have found rest, solace and affection. Her mother, busy calculating the extent of Camille's disgrace, blamed and condemned her. Her sister, Louise, never particularly indulgent by nature, had watched the blossoming of her sister's talent and her success in Paris with scorn. Now she triumphed. At the time, too, distances were huge obstacles. The one person close to Camille, her brother—who loved and understood her—was absent. From 1895 to 1909 (except for three brief holiday trips in 1895, 1900 and 1905), Paul Claudel was far from Europe. This separation of brother from sister during the most painful time in Camille's life, a time when she most required tenderness and help, must have been for her a determining factor. Alone, old Louis-Prosper, her father, helped Camille secretly by sending her some money. Over and over, Camille blamed Rodin for all her troubles: "He uses my own [family] to inflict his vengeance. To let me end my career at the mercy of my family, what gall!" she wrote in 1905 in a letter to Paul.[*]

Of Camille's last sad years, one of her few remaining friends, Henry Asselin, left a moving account:

> One morning when I went to her to pose, the door was only opened after a lengthy confabulation: at last, I was in the presence of a gloomy Camille who, untidy and trembling with fear, was armed with the handle of a broom spiked with nails. She said to me: "This night, two individuals

[*] Claudel Fund, Bibliothèque Nationale.

66

tried to force open my shutters. I recognized them: they are two of Rodin's Italian models. He ordered them to kill me. I bother him: he wants me to disappear." The persecution complex that slowly and cruelly was undermining her reason had made alarming progress over that night.

From that moment on [1905], each summer Camille would systematically destroy with hammer blows all her work of that year. Both her studios offered up a pathetic spectacle of ruin and devastation. Then, she would send for a carter to whom she gave the job of burying, somewhere in the fortifications, that shapeless and miserable debris. After which, she stuck her keys under the mat and disappeared for long months at a time without leaving an address. Paul Claudel had gone back to China. I, myself, was in Tchentou, deep in Se-Tchouen, when I received a letter from Camille which began with these words: "Your bust is no more, it lived the life of roses . . ."

When she does manage to get a bit of money, she invites a whole mob of strange people, and they drink all night laughing like children. Isn't that a sign that a little help, happiness, friendship might have, who knows, still saved her?[*]

Nevertheless, the world did not quite forget Camille Claudel. In 1906, Marguerite Durand, the founder of the newspaper *La Fronde,* wanted to publish an article by Judith Cladel on Camille. Camille was thrilled by the news: here was a little bit of light in her life. But in a letter to Marguerite Durand, Camille could not resist the temptation of slipping in some rather bitter remarks about Rodin. On the other hand, Camille showed a remarkable lack of self-interest by praising the merits of the works of another female artist, a sculptor like herself, and by suggesting that the newspaper reproduce the other woman's works rather than her own.

I am sending along the only two photographs which I was able to find. The one in the big gray coat is all right and hasn't been published. Please return them to me after you have used them.

L'Age mûr was already photographed. Last year in the article by M. André Mira, you will find it there, but it is already well known. It would be better to reproduce the work of Madame Oulmont which is very interesting and unknown.

I am in no state to be photographed at present. I've just been ill. I

---

[*] H. Asselin, "La Vie douloureuse de Camille Claudel, sculpteur" ("The Sad Life of Camille Claudel, the Sculptor"), conference on Radio Télévision Française, 1956.

look disheveled and I have nothing becoming to wear. I forgot to tell you that I would be pleased if you did an article on me but on the express condition that I will not be linked with another artist unknown to me (one of M. Rodin's protégés for whom I will act as a sort of tugboat as usual). The proximity of certain people does not please me at all.

I am happy to learn from you that something good is being prepared for me; if one could begin by paying me for the state commission* which was delivered a week ago and about which I have no news, that certainly would be wonderful."†

By 1907, the article still had not been published, and on June 2 of that year, Camille wrote Marguerite Durand again. This time, her tone was frankly disagreeable:

I've been a bit slow about answering the questions you asked me. First of all, I was and continue to be very ill. I stay in bed three quarters of the time. I only feel well when I'm lying down. I have no one to whom to give a letter so you must not be surprised by my negligence. The questions you ask me seem to me to be trifling and unnecessary for your article: why must one know who owned my sculptures?

You have plenty to say with what I told you on your last visit that is much more interesting than to enumerate unimportant details. Thus, I found it unnecessary to answer you.

Camille Claudel's last exhibition at Eugène Blot was that same year. Afterwards, she no longer appeared in public, and she was no longer seen with her old friends, the Schwobs and the Potterchers.

In 1909, Paul Claudel wrote in his journal: "In Paris, Camille mad . . . huge and looking filthy, speaking incessantly in a monotonous and metallic voice."‡ Then, in 1911, these two crossed-out lines: "November 27, Camille, at four o'clock in the morning, ran away from home, we don't know where she is."

L'Ile St. Louis had become a prison instead of a haven, and according to Paul Claudel, "The tenants of that old house on Quai Bourbon complain.

---

* The statue referred to is *The Wounded Niobide* (*La Niobide blessée*).
† Bibliothèque Marguerite Durand.
‡ Paul Claudel, *Journal I* (Paris: Gallimard, 1968), pages 103–104.

68

What was this apartment on the ground floor with the shutters always closed? Inside, the mess and the filth were, as one says, indescribable. On the walls, pinned up with tacks, the fourteen Stations of the Cross borrowed from the frontpiece of a newspaper from rue Bayard."[*]

In truth, Camille was committing suicide bit by bit. She had destroyed her work, her inner resources to work, her loves and friendships, her family ties. Camille was now nothing more than an anxious shadow hiding in the recesses of her dark studio asking only for silence and oblivion. The ultimate decision to lead her gently toward her second death at the hands of the cruel medical and administrative machinery had to be made. And so, Paul Claudel wrote, "One had to intervene . . . and there it is for thirty years."[†]

[*] Paul Claudel, Preface to the *Catalogue de L'Exposition Camille Claudel.* Musée Rodin, 1951.
[†] Ibid.

Chapter 4

The Living Death (1913-1943)

Once I was happy; I was beautiful. But
  all of a sudden
Everything broke like a mirror, as if
  a single day announced
That memory was dead among the blind!

Paul Claudel, *Tête d'or*

Who decided to commit Camille and how? These are questions without answers since almost all the correspondence has been destroyed. In his *Journal*, Paul Claudel is nearly as silent as the grave on personal matters. The artist's biographer has to rely on deduction. Here is a record of the sequence of events:

Sunday, March 2, 1913: death of Louis-Prosper Claudel at three o'clock in the morning in Villeneuve.

Tuesday, March 4: burial in Villeneuve. Camille is not informed and is absent.

Wednesday, March 5: Paul Claudel meets with a Dr. Michaux, whose office happens to be at 19 Quai Bourbon. The doctor gives him a medical certificate which authorizes internment according to the law of 1838.[*]

---

[*] The law of 1838, still in force today, stated that patients could be confined on the basis of a simple medical certificate. They were then put under the jurisdiction of the institution's doctor and he, in turn, had the power to allow them to leave.

Friday, March 7: Paul Claudel meets the director of Ville d'Évrard, who already has the doctor's certificate. He suggests a correction in the text.

Saturday, March 8: Paul Claudel writes so that the corrected certificate will arrive in time to proceed with the internment on the same day. The certificate does not reach the doctor in time. Camille spends her last Sunday in Paris.

Monday, March 10: Camille is interned. Two muscular male nurses force their way into her studio on Quai Bourbon and bodily take her away.

There is no question that the haste with which Camille was incarcerated was shocking. Paul Claudel himself notes in his *Journal,* "I've been very unhappy this week."[*] The temptation, too, is to interpret the act as one of bourgeois revenge: rigid moral standards stuffed with uncharitable Catholicism versus the artistic life, genius and dreams. But how could Paul Claudel, suddenly become the head of the family, have complied with the machinations of jealous women when by all indications his love for his sister never varied, would, in fact, never vary? Their correspondence was never interrupted. During each of his trips to France, Paul went to see Camille in the asylum. He was the only member of the family to visit Camille and comfort her.

The polemics on the abusive nature of her incarceration soon began. On September 19, 1913, *L'Avenir de l'Aisne,* an anticlerical daily, published an article entitled "Our Compatriots":

> The work of a brilliant sculptor, originally a native of this region, reviewed by a great poet is what *L'Art décoratif* offers us in a special issue in which Paul Claudel analyzes the powerful and vibrant art of his sister, Camille Claudel.
>
> This astonishing artist, battered repeatedly by cruel destiny, was still waiting for the moment when tardy justice would make her the equal of the greatest plastic artists. Thanks to *L'Art décoratif,* this moment has arrived; those who saw the forty-eight reproductions (one of which, *hors texte,* is in color), assembled by M. Fernand Hoches, will learn to appreciate this work in which the nobility of Donatello has been brought

[*] Paul Claudel, *Journal I,* page 247.

alive by a totally modern spirit and they will not hesitate to salute Camille Claudel as the veritable sculptor of our time. However, a monstrous and unheard-of thing [has occurred]: while in full possession of her great talent and of her intellectual faculties, some men arrived at her door, brutally and despite her indignant protests threw her into a car, so that to this day, this great artist is locked up in a lunatic asylum. Can't *L'Avenir de l'Aisne* of Chateau-Thierry, in the interest of justice and to respect individual liberty, give us some information about this unjustifiable abduction and this incarceration which constitute the most monstrous crime in a country that considers itself civilized? What is so frightening is that while crimes occur everyday and go unpunished, thanks to the law of 1838 concerning the insane, the Catholic Church and the soldiery can do whatever they like regardless of the laws; one leaves them strictly alone, they are taboo and beyond the law.

Early newspaper accounts did not directly blame the Claudel family but everything changed once the Parisian press got hold of the affair. Paul Vibert, a journalist for the *Grand National,* condemned the law of 1838 in an editorial on December 8, 1913. Referring to this article, *L'Avenir de l'Aisne* published another unsigned piece in its local news section on December 12, 1913. The inhabitants of Villeneuve-sur-Fère had little trouble recognizing the leading players in the drama:

An incarceration of a very subtle sort has just taken place in Paris. A mother and a brother have managed to sequester Mlle. C., an artist of great talent. The poor daughter had just barely and by chance learned of the opportune death of her father, who loved her dearly and whose death had been hidden from her, when, the day after the news and while she was overwhelmed and stricken with grief, two strong fellows broke into her room around eleven o'clock in the morning, grabbed her and, despite her protestations and her tears, took her away to an asylum. Three days later, the poor woman wrote: "I have to my credit thirty years of strenuous work and all the same I am punished; they keep a tight hold over me and I won't get out."
    A little later, the internment was converted into a sequestration. That's how one gets rid of a healthy mind in society.

On December 17, 1913, Paul Vibert beseeched Paul Claudel "to enlighten public opinion, which was beginning to express uneasiness about such

72

crimes. . . ." On December 20, the article made a point-blank accusation: Camille Claudel, "absolutely sane of mind and body," was seized at home by three men without an official mandate, in violation of her rights of domicile, and was thrown into a car headed for the asylum at Ville-Évrard.

Paul Claudel did not respond to the attacks. Since October 1913 he had been consul-general in Hamburg, and although he was well aware of the attacks, his official position forbade him to reply to them. In his *Journal,* he wrote: "Horrible slanders against us regarding Camille's internment at Ville-Évrard from Lelm and the Thierrys in *L'Avenir de l'Aisne* and other extortionist papers denouncing a 'clerical crime.' That is fine. I've received so much undeserved praise that slander is refreshing and good, it's the normal lot of a Christian."[*] Later, in his preface to the catalog of the 1951 Camille Claudel exhibition, he changed the dates and wrote that she was interned in July of 1913. Was that intentional?

It was Camille Claudel herself who lit the powder keg. On March 10, 14 and 21, 1913, she wrote three letters in pencil to her cousin Charles Thierry. The first one is dated on the very day that she was incarcerated.

March 10

My dear Charles,
You send me the news of Papa's death; this is the first I've heard of it, no one told me. When did it happen? Try to find out and give me some details. Poor Papa, he never saw me the way I really am; everyone always tried to make him believe that I was an odious, mean and ungrateful creature; that was necessary so that the other one could take it all.

I had to disappear as quickly as I could and even though I try to make myself as small as possible in my corner, I am still in the way. They have already tried to lock me up in a lunatic asylum for fear that I will harm little Jacques[†] by claiming my rights. That's what would happen if I were unlucky enough to step foot there. Louise has her hands on all the family money with the help of her friend, Rodin,[‡] while I myself am always in need of a little money, little though it may be I still need a bit, and it is I who am despised when I ask for some. These things are done on purpose because as you know Louise spends much time with the Protestants.

[*] Paul Claudel, *Journal I,* page 268.
[†] Jacques de Massary, Louise Claudel's son.
[‡] The accusation is absurd, considering how much the Claudel family hated Rodin.

73

I wouldn't dare go to Villeneuve, and I would have to be able to go, I don't have any money, not even some shoes. I've been put on short rations, sorrow is my lot. If you know something tell me; I will not risk writing, I'll be snubbed as usual.

I am astonished that Papa died; he should have lived to be a hundred. There is something at the bottom of this. My best regards to you and Emma.

K-mille [*sic*]

March 14

My dear Charles,
My letter of the other day was like a forewarning for barely was it posted than an automobile came for me at home to take me to an asylum. I am or, at least, I think I am at the asylum of Ville-Évrard. If you can come to see me, you can take your time about it, I am not about to get out; they hold me and they don't want to let me go.

If you can bring me a picture of my aunt* to keep me company you would give me great pleasure. You won't recognize me, you who saw me so young and radiant in the salon at Chacrise. . . .†

March 21

My dear Charles,
You have no idea of the pleasure you give me by sending the picture of my aunt and of Mme. du Jay; I will never leave them again. Poor women, they were so good, so unassuming, one felt happy with them. Ah! If they were alive today, I would not be the way I am; they were so generous. You are kind to give up something for my sake. You are always ready to make me happy. That is just like your mother; if you were still the owner, I would immediately move in with you at Chacrise. Forget all this.

If Jeanne were alive, I don't know what could have happened to her, I wouldn't be like this, she was so good to me. You know that Alfred lives close by in Pavillon-sous-Bois. Paul Cookborn also, a friend of Monsieur Marcy, is in Montreuil-sous-Bois. They came to see me at my studio. I wait impatiently for your visit even under these circumstances.

I am not reassured, I don't know what will happen to me. I feel as if things are about to end badly for me, all this strikes me as underhand, if you were in my place, you would see. It was well worth my while to

---

* Julienne du Jay, born in Chacrise, Aisne. She married Joseph-Charles Thierry and thus was Camille's aunt; she was also Camille's godmother.
† The du Jay property.

74

have worked so hard and to have had some talent to be rewarded like this. Never a sou, tormented every which way all my life. Deprived of everything that makes one glad to be alive and still end up like this.

Do you remember the poor Marquis du Sauvencourt from the Château du Muret, your ex-neighbor? He only died just now after being locked up for thirty years! It's horrible and one can't imagine it. Give my greetings to your dear Emma, to your daughter and to your children; I send you my best regards. . . . *

If Camille was not mad, as Vibert maintained, her internment was odious, illegal and criminal. What is the truth of the matter? The first signs of Camille's emotional imbalance occurred right after she broke off with Rodin around 1893. In his remarkable study of Camille in the *Mercure de France*, Mathias Morhardt, her fervent admirer, mentioned her taste for solitude and her distrust of strangers. Camille's determination to shut herself off also worried her father. In 1904, he hesitated to accept the invitation of his relative Marie Merklen† to spend the September holidays in Gérardmer because he did not want to leave Camille alone. "It was very kind of you," he wrote, "but it would be with a heavy heart that I would abandon Camille in her isolation."‡ There are other witnesses, such as Dr. Michaux, who is of special interest because he was the son of the Dr. Michaux who filled out the medical certificate needed to intern Camille. He wrote the following letter on December 18, 1951, to Professor Mondor:

A few months ago, I read your book on Paul Claudel. The chapter that deals with Camille Claudel evoked my childhood memories. Camille Claudel lived on the ground floor of 19 Quai Bourbon where my father practiced medicine for fifty-five years. In back of the courtyard, there was a garden which belonged to Maurice Maindron and where a great many academic dinners took place under the aegis of Heredia. The courtyard was my playground. My parents forbade me to go to Camille Claudel's (to whom we were vaguely and distantly related). They were afraid that I would enter this Capernaum where a virgin forest of spider webs had accumulated in the midst of busts and the comings and goings of at least a dozen cats.

---

* These letters were made available through the kindness of Mme. Suzanne Mulsant, *née* Massary.
† Marie Merklen was the first cousin and godmother of Paul Claudel.
‡ Louis-Prosper Claudel's letter to his son. *Cahiers Paul Claudel*, No. 1 (Paris: Gallimard, 1959), page 116.

But the lure of the forbidden fruit reinforced by my own taste for cats as well as that for the proffered sweets made me brave these interdictions. It was there that I got my first lesson in psychiatry, and I cannot speak or write about psychotic paranoia without thinking of my disheveled neighbor in her white dressing gown who spoke about "that scoundrel of a Rodin" while he, to my ten-year-old eyes, took on the proportions of a mythological character.*

Camille's last letters—the ones she wrote during her last years of freedom as well as those she wrote during the early months in the asylum and before a claim can be made that she was contaminated by the constant presence of madmen—also testify to the ravages of a morbid obsession whose focus is Rodin: the whole world persecuted her, fortunes worth millions (millions in terms of 1913) were built on her works. The extracts from a letter Camille wrote Paul around 1910 are particularly significant:

Don't take my sculptures to Prague, I absolutely don't want to exhibit in that country. Admirers of that caliber don't interest me in the least. I would like to have the recognition for *L'Aurore* soon and as it is only fifteen francs, I will withdraw it next month and I will try to sell it. Send it back to me as soon as possible. You are right, justice is of no use against M. Hébrardt and thieves of his sort, what one needs against that type of person is a revolver, the sole and only argument. That's what one would need, mark my words, because letting someone like him go unpunished encourages the others who blatantly show my work and make money from it, under the direction of M. Rodin. But what is funnier still is that last year he dared show an *Aurore* in Italy that had my signature but which was not mine and, to push the irony to the limit, he arranged for it to win the gold medal.

I have him by the ear now. The rogue lays his hands on my statues by different means, he gives them to his pals, the chic artists, who, in turn, distribute the decorations and the ovations. When he returned, he ruined [illegible word] and made 300,000 francs with the tapestries. He did not waste any time arranging with Collin to have me come to Paris. My so-called vocation has paid off well for him!†

According to Camille, it was Rodin who had her imprisoned. He wanted to keep his fame untarnished by hers. Even her oldest friends were not

* Claudel Fund, Bibliothèque Nationale.
† Ibid.

spared, and she believed that Philippe Berthelot was part of the plot.[*] Only Eugène Blot and Paul Claudel were allowed to escape her misguided accusations. Her faithful friends had no illusions about the severity of her state. In a letter to Rodin dated June 5, 1914, Mathias Morhardt wrote: "I've just seen M. Philippe Berthelot, to whom, in a strictly confidential manner, I spoke about your wishes concerning that poor and admirable artist. He will appraise the situation very discreetly and we will come and see you together as soon as we have an exact idea of the way things are. But I insisted very firmly to Philippe Berthelot so that we would, above all, unify our efforts—all hope of a cure being ephemeral—with a view to giving adequate homage in memory of this great artist."[†]

In September 1914, Camille was transferred to the asylum of Montdevergues in the parish of Montfavet near Avignon. She was never to leave Montdevergues. To the last of her days, she was conscious of her sad fate, and for a long time she tried to escape it. Camille sent secret appeals for help to her family and to relatives. In 1918, not having understood that he was the author of her misfortunes, Camille wrote to Dr. Michaux:

6–25–1918

Doctor Sir,
Perhaps you no longer remember your ex-patient and neighbor Mlle. Claudel who was taken from her home on March 2, 1913,[‡] and carried off to lunatic asylums from where she may never again leave. For five years, nearly six, I have endured this terrible martyrdom. First, I was taken to the lunatic asylum of Ville-Évrard, then, from there, to Montdevergues near Montfavet (Vaucluse). Useless to describe to you what I have suffered. Not long ago, I wrote to M. Adam, to whom you were kind enough to recommend me and who, in the past, was able to plead successfully in my favor. I beseech him to pay attention to my case. In this circumstance, your good advice would be necessary to me as you are a man of great experience and as a medical doctor you are familiar with the question. I beg that you will be disposed to speak about me with M. Adam and to think about what you can do to help me. On

---

[*] Because of his friendship with Paul Claudel and his admiration for Camille's work, Philippe Berthelot agreed to join the family council that was formed after Camille's internment.
[†] Claudel Fund, Bibliothèque Nationale.
[‡] Camille confused the date of her incarceration with that of the death of her father.

my family's side, there is nothing one can do; under evil influences, my mother, my brother and my sister only listen to the slander that has been heaped on me.

They reproach me (O terrible crime) of living all alone, of spending my life with cats, of having a persecution complex! It's on the basis of these accusations that I've been incarcerated for the past five and a half years like a criminal, deprived of freedom, deprived of food, of heat and of most of the basic comforts. In a long letter, I have explained to M. Adam the other motives which contributed to my incarceration. I beg that you will read the letter carefully so that you can understand all the details in this affair.

Perhaps as a doctor of medicine you could use your influence in my favor. In any case, if I cannot regain my freedom right away, I would prefer to be transferred to the Salpêtrière or to Sainte-Anne or to an ordinary hospital where you could come and see me and judge for yourself the state of my health. Here, they give me 150 francs a month and one should see how I am looked after; my relatives don't pay any attention to me and only answer my pleas with a stubborn silence; thus, they do with me what they will. It is terrible to be so abandoned. I can't help but succumb to the grief that overwhelms me. Finally, I hope you can do something to help me and it goes without saying that if you have some expenses you will be good enough to keep track of them and I shall reimburse you in full. I hope that you did not have to suffer in the trenches. . . .

There is something else I want to ask you, that is, when you see the Merklen family, to tell everyone what has become of me. Mother and my sister have given instructions that I be confined in the most absolute fashion, none of my letters leave, no visitor enters.

By means of all this, my sister has gotten hold of my inheritance and she is determined that I never leave prison. Also, I beg you not to write to me here and not to say that I have written you as I write in secret against the rules of the establishment and if they knew they would make me pay for it dearly. . . .

I beg you to do what you can for me as, several times, you have shown me that you have a great deal of discretion and I put my trust in you. I have to warn you about the nonsense that is used to prolong my sequestration. They claim that they will keep me locked up until the end of the war: it is a joke and a way of deceiving me with false promises for that war will never end and by that time I'll be finished myself; ah! if you knew what one has to endure! It would make you tremble! If at some point I can no longer write to you, would you nevertheless not abandon me, and if you can, act as quickly as possible;

the impediment in this circumstance is the secret influence of strangers who have taken possession of my studio and who hold Mother in their clutches to keep her from coming to see me.[*]

From the asylum, Camille wrote letters to her mother, her brother, her friend Maria Paillette and Eugène Blot. This correspondence—taking into account the excesses caused by her psychosis—reveals a sharp mind, a memory that is intact and shows that with the passage of years Camille grew more accepting of her sufferings. Rage had turned into resignation and when she asked to leave the asylum, she was contemplating a solitary retreat in Villeneuve rather than a life in society or resuming her artistic career. Everything seemed to confirm that, deep down, Camille had abdicated; her life no longer interested her. Bit by bit, too, she resigned herself to wait for death at Montdevergues. Instead of more comfort, she longed for more silence. She accepted her condition without complaint and she categorically refused to be moved to "first class," where, according to her, the food was appalling and the inmates frightful. But isn't this cenobitic attitude common to great artists who have renounced their art?

The rest of Camille's correspondence speaks for itself. The letters are more than mere documents; they are like windows thrown open on human misery. And because her family has agreed to lift the veil of secrecy surrounding her medical condition, a diagnosis of her ailment is now possible. The facts are as follows:

Camille was neither aggressive nor violent. She never had to undergo any painful medical treatments. According to witnesses, in the course of time, she became gentler and more subdued.[†] Until 1938, the asylum was run by nuns. Sister Saint-Hubert of the parish of Saint-Charles in Lyons remembered taking care of Camille and was the only remaining witness who could be questioned about everyday life at the asylum. Mademoiselle Claudel, she said, was so silent and diminished that she virtually passed unnoticed. More than just resigned, she was amorphous. Besides, she was confined to the nonviolent section where the inmates did not need any

[*] Claudel Fund, Bibliothèque Nationale.
[†] From the letter of the chaplain of Montdevergues to Paul Claudel on October 20, 1943. Cited by Paul Claudel, *Journal II*, page 464.

surveillance or special help except to get dressed in the morning and at night. No one knew that she had been a great sculptor. Her only title was that she was Paul Claudel's sister. According to the nun, the facilities at Montdevergues were decent. The food was plentiful and adequate, and the staff ate it as well. No communal activities were ever organized, and since the inmates had few visitors, they suffered from enormous mental deprivation, which only the often silent care of the sisters mitigated. There was never any question, Sister Saint-Hubert said, of reintegrating Camille into society, although the doctors wished for patients on the road to recovery to leave in order to provide more room in an overcrowded establishment.

Since all of Camille's letters appear sensible, they are apt to arouse suspicion among those who do not realize that madness is not necessarily a permanent state. Antonin Artaud, for example, wrote beautiful letters to his friends from an asylum.

What went on in that poor woman's head for thirty years? We know nothing of how Camille spent her time except that she never sculpted: the clay that, from time to time, the establishment provided for her dried up instantly.[*] Did she read? Did she dream? We have no idea. Camille had few visitors. Her mother never came to see her—she was content to send parcels. Her sister, Louise, never came either. In answer to Camille's letters, her mother, who never forgave her her escapade with Rodin, replied harshly, first addressing the letters to the director of the asylum. She could hardly restrain herself from treating Camille like a prostitute, which obviously was not the way to help a confused mind. Fairly quickly, Camille convinced herself that her mother and her sister had conspired to put her away so that they could inherit her money. Camille's asylum fees were paid for by her mother, later by Paul Claudel, and still later with her share of the inheritance. A small portion of Camille's fees was also paid by a Beaux-Arts fund established by Rodin with the assistance of Mathias Morhardt, who took infinite pains to keep Rodin's donation anonymous. Otherwise, the Claudel family would have refused to accept a contribution from "the monster." In any event, the sum in question was only 500 francs and compared to the gigantic profits of the house of Rodin and Cie[†] (prior to the

---

[*] From a letter to Paul Claudel from the director of the Montdevergues asylum in 1943. Family Archives.
[†] I. Jianou, *Rodin* (Paris: Arted, 1980), page 104.

80

war, a bust in bronze sold for around 30,000 francs) was hardly more than a slight acknowledgment of sadness felt by the old master for his unforgettable muse. True, by then Rodin was very old and stood ready to renew his gesture.[*]

After Rodin died, the enemy, for Camille, became her mother. In turn, Louise Claudel has been accused of being an unnatural mother. Her attitude toward her incarcerated daughter was characterized by bitter animosity and appears unjustified under the circumstances. How did she really feel toward Camille? Louise Claudel was never particularly affectionate with any of her children. In keeping with the mentality of the time, she raised them from a sense of duty rather than with any love. Her principles were rigid and austere, and when Camille rejected them that was the source of the mutual misunderstanding between mother and daughter. Camille chose another way—the hazardous route of creativity and freedom. The language and gestures of love that had been denied her in life she sought in art. Louise Claudel remained totally oblivious to Camille's conflicts. Narrow-minded, she never even tried to see or understand them. Her traditions, her preconceived notions were for her universal truths. After she had played the dutiful role of mother, she assumed her part was finished and it was up to others to take responsibility for her daughter. The correspondence between Louise Claudel and the director of the asylum reveals a helplessness that took the form of a mental block: she neither could nor wanted to intervene and she must have guessed the outcome. In 1915 she wrote the director of the asylum of Montdevergues:

> At no cost do I want to remove her from your establishment where she was content not too long ago. I will not have her changing establishments every six months and as far as taking her back with me or sending her back home like she was, never, never. I am 75 years old, I cannot take care of a daughter who has the most absurd ideas, who wishes us ill, who hates us and is ready to do us all the evil she can. If one has to pay an additional fee for her board so that she will be more comfortable, I don't ask for anything better, but keep her, I beg you. At home, she lived like a destitute person, she hadn't seen a single soul in the past 10 years, she was robbed by everyone who sold food to her. The doors and windows were chained, padlocked, and whatever she ate was put

[*] Letters of Rodin and M. Morhardt. Claudel Fund, Bibliothèque Nationale.

81

in a packing case on top of one of the windows. As for her person and her apartment, it was something horrible. She spent her time writing letters to good-for-nothings and making denunciations. In short, she has all the vices, I don't want to see her again, she has done us too much harm.[*]

"Camille has brought this trouble on herself," Louise Claudel wrote in another letter. "I don't have any authority over her and I would have to suffer all her whims, never would I consent to this arrangement. She has pulled the wool over our eyes for too long."[†]

Despite their bitterness, these letters are somewhat pitiful. We can guess that the old woman was making a desperate last stand in self-defense. She was trying to hold on to her old convictions. Camille's freedom would have been like her death sentence. "One cannot allow those who suffer from a persecution complex freedom without grave danger," she said.

In spite of their lack of understanding and warmth, Louise Claudel's letters also show her constant preoccupation with trying to better her daughter's lot. She regularly sent Camille parcels, even during the most difficult periods, and never did money questions interfere with her relations with her daughter or with the asylum's administration. Only once were financial issues raised: when the house and property at Villeneuve were ravaged by the war and Madame Claudel was reduced to her widow's pension: "You know that on account of the war, I have lost almost everything I owned and now I have to wait a few years for the war damages that I've been promised as well as those from the Russian front."[‡]

As for Camille's letters to her mother, they revealed the same obsession. "She continues," wrote her mother, "to treat us like thieves who turned over her studio which was filled with works of art to her enemies and of having thrown out into the dump all her boxes which, among other things, contained a monument of Victor Hugo, a group of *Gossipers,* etc., while, in fact, the cases were filled with nothing more than packages of shapeless clay which we had a lot of trouble getting rid of. It is impossible to

[*] From Louise Claudel's letter to the director of the Montdevergues Asylum. Archives of the Montdevergues Asylum.
[†] Ibid.
[‡] Archives of the Montdevergues Asylum.

82

believe that she has a healthy mind and that she can behave reasonably, no more so now than when she first entered the home for mental patients in which, no longer able to cope with her incoherencies, we had to place her."*

Faced with these facts, what was the reasonable solution? It was impossible to let Camille take care of herself, and, old and sick, her mother could not take on the responsibility. Instead of getting better, Camille's obsession had worsened. In May 1915, she wrote her brother about how Rodin and his friends were persecuting and stealing from her: "Have you looked after my things that you told me you stored in Villeneuve? Have you made sure that they haven't fallen into the hands of the friends of that scoundrel who dealt me this pretty blow so that he could take them? He is scared silly to see me return before he has had the time to get his hands on. . . . That is why he keeps delaying for as long as possible my getting out; he is trying to gain time and in the interval, all sorts of things are going to happen that you don't expect. You will be punished for your apathy; so beware."†

Later, Camille persuaded herself that they were trying to kill her. She refused the food of the "first class" so as not to eat from the communal kitchen, where she thought the food was designed to poison her. She was determined to keep cooking her own potatoes and eggs. In short, a solution within the family was unthinkable. Her brother was abroad; Camille could not live with him. She even turned to her sister. In a letter to Paul, Camille proposed to give her nephew, Jacques de Massary, a gift as a form of damage payment. "You can tell Mother that if she is afraid that I will claim the Villeneuve property, I have no such intention; I would prefer to make a gift to Jacques of everything I inherit and spend the rest of my life in peace."‡ But her protestations were a waste of time. Her sister did not love her, and it is hard to picture that poor hapless creature returning to be at the mercy of the family. In the end, it was always to Paul that Camille turned, and he, in turn, always responded to her calls. Even while he was having his own financial difficulties, he never stopped trying to inter-

---

* Archives of the Montdevergues Asylum.
† Ibid.
‡ Ibid.

vene on Camille's behalf and for her comfort by sending her money.[*]

The years passed without diminishing the hatreds. Camille's mother died in 1929. Everyone lived his own life, the family council deliberated, and Camille's board was duly paid as she slowly made her way to her second death. Toward the end of 1942, the asylum doctor noted a failure in her general health—senility.[†] Little by little, Camille was declining, and in September 1943 Paul Claudel was alerted. With great difficulty, he crossed Occupied France to see her once more and for the last time. Through his tears, he recognized underneath an old bonnet "that skull that like a neglected monument reveals its magnificent architecture"—the last vestige of a superb young woman. Camille died on October 19, 1943, an old, miserable, unknown woman. Far from her native soil, her body was disposed of by the authorities, a final and poignant symbol of her neglected life.

Camille Claudel was buried in the cemetery of Montfavet, in a section reserved for the inmates of the Montdevergues Asylum. When the war was over, her nephew attempted to have the body brought back to the family tomb in Villeneuve to give it a more dignified resting place. He came up against the impossible—Camille's grave turned out to be public and anonymous. Instead, a commemorative plaque was placed in the church of Villeneuve above the tomb of the Claudel-Massary family—as if, in the end, Camille herself had erased all her own traces, leaving only her name and her work.

In the ensuing years Camille Claudel's work was exhibited on occasion. The Musée Rodin opened its doors to her (although the "Camille Claudel Room" that Rodin and Morhardt had hoped for did not materialize),[‡] and in 1935, her work was honored in the Exposition des Femmes Artistes Modernes. Her name is included in histories of art, although Bénézit's *Dictionnaire des peintres, sculpteurs, dessinateurs et graveurs* delicately lists her death as occurring in 1920.

---

[*] Paul Claudel did not become an ambassador until 1922. Before then he lived quite modestly.

[†] Letter from the director of the Montdevergues Asylum to Paul Claudel. Claudel Fund, Bibliothèque Nationale.

[‡] Correspondence between M. Morhardt and A. Rodin. Claudel Fund, Bibliothèque Nationale.

Chapter 5

When We Dead Awaken

In 1899 Henrik Ibsen published his last play, *When We Dead Awaken*—three short, dense acts with four characters. It is a typical, if not outright predictable, drama in which the protagonist, Professor Rubek, is a famous sculptor. One feels certain that the play was inspired by the liaison between Auguste Rodin and Camille Claudel.

Early on in his career, Rodin was well known in Norway. Norway's national sculptor, Gustav Vigeland, a friend of Ibsen's, worked in Paris for a long time and not far from the French master whose art greatly influenced him. Another friend of Ibsen's, the painter Fritz Thaulow,[*] lived in Paris. He met with Rodin and Camille often, and even bought several of Camille's works, one of them the original plaster of *The Waltz*. Thus, a chain of events links the biographical facts with literary fiction, although Ibsen never knew Rodin personally.

In terms of Camille's destiny, the play, written in 1899, is a dark prophecy and sheds some light for us on the workings of Rodin's mind. A brief summary of the plot follows.

Professor Rubek, basking in his fame, is vacationing at a seaside resort

---

[*] Two of his paintings are in the Rodin Museum—a part of Rodin's collection.

with his wife, Maia, a strong-willed, matter-of-fact young woman—a younger, prettier version of Rose Beuret. Rubek is tired and can only sculpt busts; the inspiration for larger works is gone. Then Irene, a woman from his past, arrives accompanied by her mute chaperone—a symbol of death. Irene tells of her sad fate as an abandoned woman made all the more pathetic since she was once the inspiration and the model for the artist's greatest work, *The Day of Resurrection*. Irene is on her way to madness. She wanders from one man to another, she has lost her children and as part of a café concert act she has even exhibited her once-magnificent body, the model for *The Resurrection*. Meanwhile, Rubek calculates the disastrous events of his life, the result of his weaknesses, and guesses that death is about to claim him. Maia, disappointed that he does not keep his promise and show her "the splendors of the earth from the top of the mountain"— Rubek is no longer capable of doing so—seeks out the bear hunter Ulfheim, a rude and violent man. Rubek and Irene see each other for the last time. Their final dialogue is filled with exaltation, remorse and madness, a sort of exacerbated examination of conscience which ends in their death, symbolized by an avalanche. Maia leaves with the bear hunter in search of a new life.

Viewed from the limited perspective of a Camille Claudel historian, Ibsen's play is like an echo of the conversations and opinions of Camille Claudel's and Rodin's circle of friends and relatives. Curious prattle, conjecture, even compassion never fail to accompany the liaisons of the famous. Ibsen reflects these murmurs, whispers them in our ears. In addition, the play emphasizes for us the bitter waste as well as the inevitability of their tragic relationship. Everything that occurs to the lovers seems ineluctable, as if at some point the mastery of their fates had escaped them, damaging them both forever.

No one will ever be able to measure accurately what is anecdote and what is creative intuition in *When We Dead Awaken*, but that does not matter. As it is, the play stands as an impressive document that dramatizes the vertiginous emotions experienced by Camille Claudel and Rodin when they separated.

38. Louise Claudel (Madame de Massary). *Pastel, around 1887,*
50½ × 36¼ inches.

39. *Study for* Çacountala. *Terra cotta, 1888,*
8¼ × 7½ × 5 inches.

40.

41.

40, 41. Death of a Little Girl with Doves. *Oil on canvas, 1898,*
49¼ × 51¼ inches.

42. The Gossipers. *Onyx and bronze, 1897,*
17³⁄₄ × 16¹⁄₄ × 13³⁄₄ inches.

*43. Woman on a Sofa. Oil on canvas, around 1900,
28½ × 36¼ inches.*

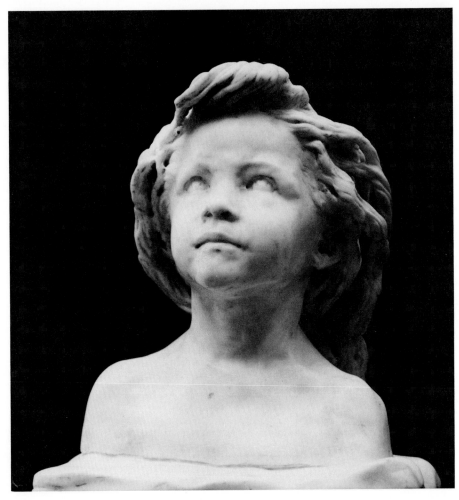

44. The Little Chatelaine. *Marble, 1896,*
17¼ × 13½ × 11¾ inches.

OPPOSITE: *45, 46.* The Wave.
Bronze and onyx, 1898,
24½ × 22 × 19¾ inches.

45.

46.

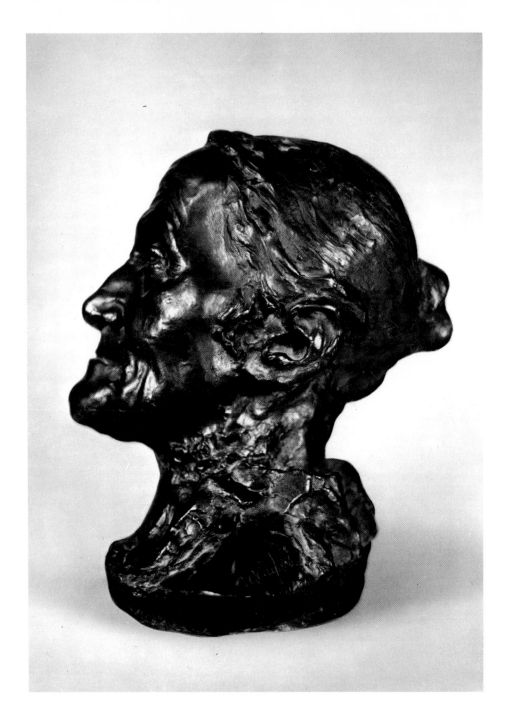

47. Old Helen. *Bronze, 1882,*
11 × 7 × 8¼ inches.

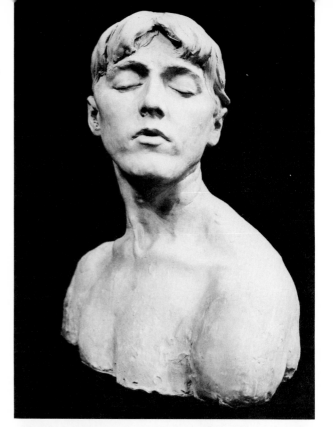

48.

49.

48, 49. Bust of a Woman
with Closed Eyes.
Terra cotta,
around 1884,
$14\frac{1}{2} \times 13\frac{3}{4} \times 7\frac{3}{4}$ *inches.*

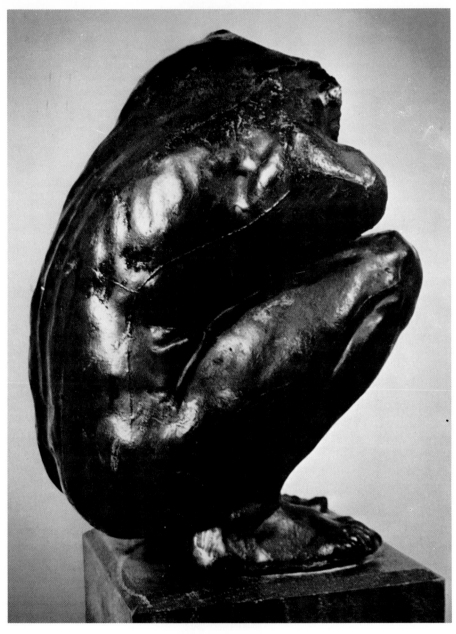

50, 51. Torso of a Crouching Woman. *Bronze, 1884,*
13³/₄ × 7³/₄ × 6 inches.

51.

52, 53. Young Roman (My Brother at Sixteen). *Bronze, 1884,*
17¼ × 17 × 9½ inches.

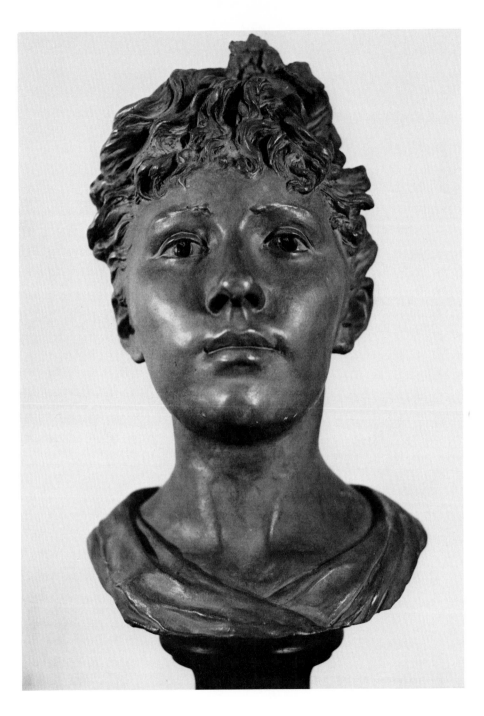

54. Bust of Louise Claudel. *Terra cotta, 1885, 19¼ × 8½ × 9¾ inches.*

55.

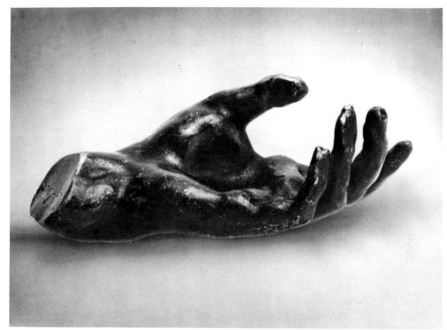

56.

55, 56. Study of a Hand. *Bronze, around 1885,*
4 × 1½ × 1½ inches.

57. Study of a Head. *Plaster, around 1885,*
5½ × 4¾ × 5½ inches.

OPPOSITE: *58.* Giganti. *Bronze, 1885,*
12½ × 10¼ × 10½ inches.

59. Man with His Arms Crossed.
Terra cotta, around 1885,
4 × 3¾ × 3¼ inches.

OPPOSITE: 60. Man Leaning. *Plaster, around 1885,*
16½ × 6¾ × 9¾ inches.

61. Young Roman. *Plaster, 1896,*
19¾ × 17¾ × 10¼ inches.

OPPOSITE: 62. Bust of Rodin. *Bronze, 1892,*
16 × 10¼ × 11 inches.

64. Çacountala. *Bronze, 1905,*
24½ × 22½ × 10½ *inches.*

OPPOSITE: 63. Çacountala. *Terra cotta, 1888,*
8¼ × 7½ × 5 *inches.*

Photos 66–72 show the marble Çacountala *in detail.*

67.

68.

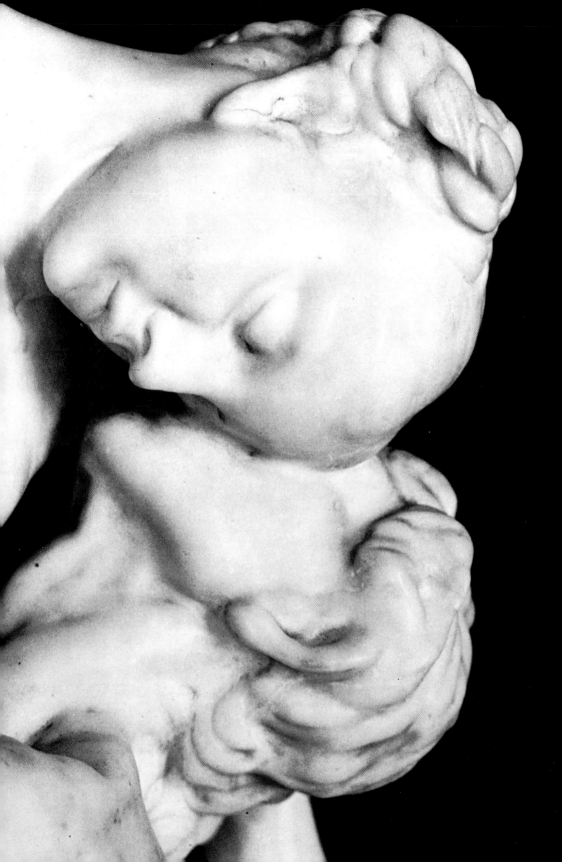

69.

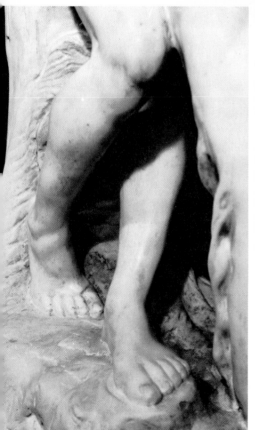

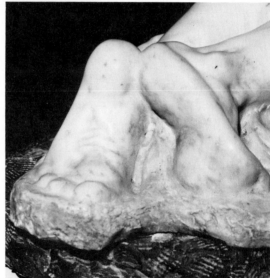

71.

70.

72.

73. Charles Lhermitte as a Child.
Bronze, 1889, 11¾ × 11¾ × 9 inches.

74.

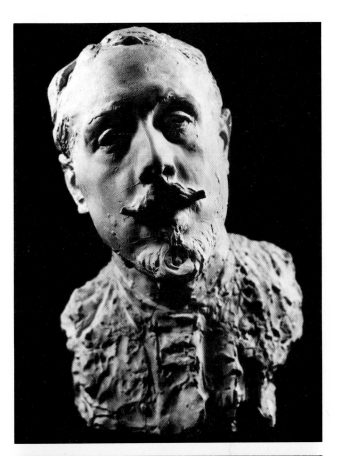

75.

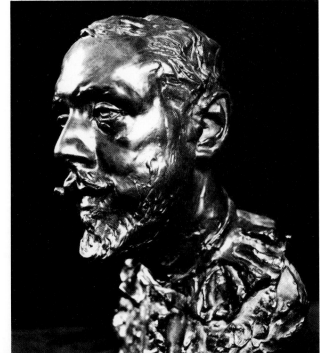

74. Ferdinand de Massary.
Plaster, 1888,
16½ × 6 × 9½ inches.

75. Ferdinand de Massary.
Bronze, 1888,
17 × 11 × 11¾ inches.

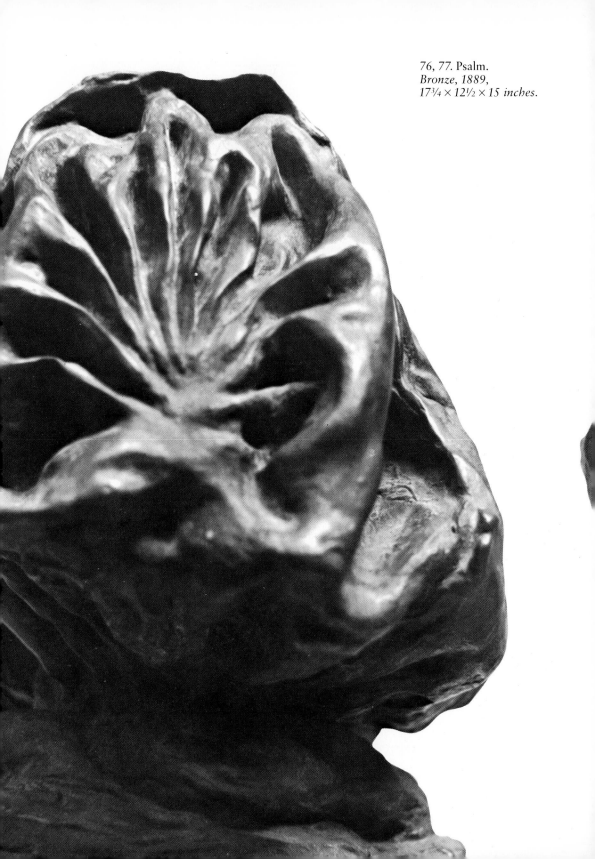

76, 77. Psalm.
Bronze, 1889,
17¾ × 12½ × 15 inches.

78, 79. Young Woman with a Sheaf.
Bronze, around 1890,
13¾ × 6¼ × 12¼ *inches.*

80, 81. The Waltz. *Bronze, 1905,*
18¼ × 12½ × 8 inches.

124

82. The Waltz *(detail)*.

83.

83, 84. Clotho. *Plaster, 1893, 35½ × 13¾ × 13¾ inches.*

84.

Chapter 6

Correspondence

Most of the letters that appear on the following pages were written by Camille Claudel from the asylum. Some of the replies are included. Although Camille's letters may not contribute a great deal to our knowledge of her art, they do acquaint us with her personal tragedy, to which it is difficult to remain indifferent. In addition, the letters complete the interior portrait of Camille Claudel by showing us her naïve and gentle nature, and her attachment to her family and to her native soil. Sadly, the letters also show to what extent she was prey to her morbid obsessions. Louise Claudel's letters to the director of the asylum reveal her own anguish and her anxiety in the face of the possibility of Camille's return to the family.

Camille Claudel to Paul Claudel. Undated. After 1907.

I tremble for the fate of *Maturity* (*Old Age*), what will happen to it, unbelievable! If I judge by what happened to *The Gossipers* shown in 1890.[*] From that very moment, various individuals used it to make themselves a profit.

---

[*] According to Mathias Morhardt, *The Gossipers* was first shown at the Salon du Champ-de-Mars in 1895. Camille mixes up the dates and the facts.

Among them, a Swedish woman (Stalkelberg de Frumerie) who, ever since, every year shows a more or less modified group of *Gossipers,* and lots of other painters and sculptors who show [illegible word]. After that, they are astonished that I shut my studio door on them and that I refuse to give them the models which benefit all but me. What a surprise. Last year, my neighbor, M. Picard, Rodin's pal and the brother of a detective, broke into my house with a passkey. Against the wall, there was a woman in yellow; since, he has made several women in yellow, the same size exactly as mine, which he has shown. Net profit: 100,000 francs. Since then, they are all making women in yellow and when I'll want to show mine, they'll take sides against me and forbid me to. On the same day, M. Picard saw a monument in my studio that I was working on and told his pals, the sculptors, one shares like brothers among Freemasons. Another year, I used a boy to bring me wood and he saw a sketch I was working on, "a woman with a doe" . . . Every Sunday, he went to Meudon to report to M. Rodin on what he had seen. The result: this year alone, there were three women with a doe in the Salon modeled after mine and life-size; profit: 100,000 francs. Another time, a cleaning woman put a drug in my coffee which put me to sleep for twelve solid hours. During that time, the woman went into my dressing room and took the woman with a cross. The result, 3 figures of women with a cross. Profit: 100,000. After that *The Little Hearth* (*La Petite cheminée*). In all of Paris, that year, one saw nothing but chimneys with a woman sitting, standing, lying down, etc. Same thing with *Maturity,* one after the other, they'll all do it. Every time I put out a model, the millions roll in for the smelters, the casters, the artists, the dealers and for me . . . $0+0=0$. That pathetic specimen of a man uses me in all sorts of ways and shares with his pals, the chic artists, while they in turn get him decorated, give him ovations, banquets, etc. . . . The ovations of this famous man have cost me an arm and a leg and I get less than nothing!!!

Since then, he has enticed the Cartereaus to Paris and stolen all their furniture. Profit: 500,000 francs. The scoundrel takes advantage of us and makes himself a nice little bundle. And when I kick out against the traces, he uses you to whip me on. The technique is simple to understand.

Keep all this to yourself, useless to speak out, better to act under cover. When they speak to you of me, you will say: "Are you surprised that she refuses that kind of system, yet it's logical enough, everyone would do the same thing, the pride of the artist is at stake, that's reasonable and nothing ever in it for her?"

And to have the gall after using my groups for more than 20 years to make me finish my career at the mercy of my family! the gall! You will tell them "You owe her something for everything you've taken away from her during these past years, otherwise her studio will henceforth remain hermetically sealed," I can't help it. The Huguenots are as clever as they are fierce. They raised me expressly to provide them with ideas knowing the emptiness of their own imaginations. I am like a cabbage that is gnawed on by caterpillars, as soon as I grow another leaf, they eat it. The ferocity of the Huguenots was legendary at the time of the Renaissance, it has not changed since.

Don't show my letter to anyone, beware of how they bribe you.

My love to you and Reine and Chouchette.*

Don't speak of anything, and above all, don't mention any names, otherwise they'll all threaten me.

Camille Claudel to Henry Lerolle. Not dated.

I sent your picture to your home so you could sign it. If you are to be absent long, please have your son sign it. To my great shame, I confess that I sold it (150 francs) as I badly needed the money: you'll forgive me won't you? you understand the desperation of artists in dire straits.

M. Rodin, whom you know, has amused himself this year by cutting off my livelihood everywhere after he forced me to leave the Salon de la Nationale out of spite.

What is more, he insults me, he publishes my portrait on postcards all over the place although I've expressly forbidden it. Nothing daunts him, he thinks he has unlimited power. All my life, I shall be hounded by that monster's vengeance.

I wanted to bring Countess Maigret to you as I had promised but in

---

* Reine was the wife of Paul Claudel; Chouchette was the nickname of Marie, Paul's eldest daughter.

the meantime, they have set her against me. My good mother who dreamt of nothing better than to put my sister in my place in that house and Lhermitte whom I kept from completely moving in there schemed so that I lost the affection of that lady, my only buyer. You see how it was not my fault.

I keep thinking of the poor welcome you got in my home thanks to the good-for-nothings that I had employed; but you who understand what fools artists are in practical matters won't hold that against me, I am sure.

If you want to come and see me, you will see the group I am finishing with the sweat of my brow, let me know with a word.

C. Claudel

Camille Claudel to Paul Claudel. Around 1910.

[The beginning is missing.]

Don't take my sculptures to Prague. I absolutely don't want to exhibit in that country. Admirers of that caliber don't interest me in the least. I would like to have the recognition for *Aurora* (*L'Aurore*) soon and as it is only fifteen francs, I will withdraw it next month and I will try to sell it. Send it back to me as soon as possible.

You are right, justice is of no use against M. Hébrardt and thieves of that sort, what one needs against that type of person is a revolver, the sole and only argument.

That's what one would need, mark my word, because letting someone like him go unpunished encourages the others who blatantly show my work and make money from it, under the direction of M. Rodin. But what is funnier still is that last year he dared show an *Aurora* in Italy that had my signature but which was not mine and, to push the irony to the limit, he arranged for it to win the gold medal.

I have him by the ear now.

The rogue lays his hands on my statues by different means, he gives them to his pals, the chic artists, who, in turn, distribute the decorations and the ovations, etc.

When he returned, he ruined [illegible word] and made 300,000 francs

132

with the tapestries. He did not waste any time arranging with Collin to have me come to Paris.

My so-called vocation has paid off well for him!

See you soon.

Camille

Camille Claudel to Henri Thierry, 1910.

Dear Henri,

I received your letter with great pleasure despite the fact that you also give me news of your bad health which affects me deeply as you represent for me everything that is still left of Chacrise* (all the others have disappeared).

You say that your stay in the hospital was not a success, is that true? They fed you a fine broth to finish you off, that's what they are doing right now: the whole French population is being decimated by the poison of the Protestants, the Freemasons, etc. . . . Those who showed themselves patriotic during the time of the Dreyfus affair especially know what they are doing. Little by little, they are substituting the German population, they bring them in secretly and in bits and pieces. If I tell you this, it's because I've often observed it. Each time a German needs a position or some property, they kill a Frenchman who is in the way. As for me, I have my share of it, I'm always sick with the poison that's in my blood, my body is burnt from it; it's the Huguenot Rodin who makes them distribute the dose to me for he hopes to inherit my studio with the help of his good friend, the lady Massary. It is because of the combined action of those two scoundrels that you see me in such a state. Long ago, they struck a bargain together in the woods of Villeneuve in which he undertook to make me disappear and to rid her of me and in which she undertook to help him lay his hands on my works just as soon as I had finished them. They sealed the bargain with some good kisses on the mouth and swore mutual friendship to each other. Since that moment, they lie in wait like

---

*Chacrise was an estate belonging to the Thierry family in the Aisne region.

133

thieves at a market to rob me of all I have. You can take comfort in that you were not the first and that you are not the last either! You can light a first-rate candle to St. Joseph for having saved you from the yellow peril! Otherwise, you would have already pirouetted to the other sides of the straits in poor Ferdinand's[*] place who because of our friend Rodin's little powders was quickly delivered from his sufferings here below. You can kiss your wife with total confidence, you haven't lost anything! I never saw Jeanne's[†] children again, they have been hooked by the Protestants, they have been riled up against me so they can lay their hands on them. That's what the Protestants always do, they get their hands on young people to turn them into sectarians. I'm always in the same state and it is that Huguenot Rodin who wages war against me with his good friend the lady Massary. At this moment, he is trying to keep Mother from paying my rent so that I shall be forced to work for nothing for that mean reformed Catholic in the convent of the Sacred Heart where he had the gall to install himself.

I fight against venom with two kinds of infusions: an infusion of plantain leaves which destroys venom; an infusion of burdock roots which purifies the kidneys. It is excellent and it relieves me enormously. I advise you to do the same and especially, never to take the medicine that the doctors prescribe, especially those that contain salicylate of soda.

I don't know when I shall be able to go and see you, Mother tells me she is arriving, she will perhaps stay a fortnight; as soon as I can bestir myself I shall go and see what has become of you. If you should die, I will shout everywhere that the Protestants poisoned you, if I die, do the same, that way they will always be at fault.

Don't show my letter to anyone, it is not worth it.

I send affectionate greetings to all of you and my good wishes for the new year.

I hope to see you soon,
Camille

[*] Ferdinand de Massary, Camille Claudel's brother-in-law.
[†] Jeanne, the daughter of Henri and Henriette Thierry.

134

*Condolence letter from Camille Claudel to Henriette Thierry
on the death of her husband. (He died in November 1912.)*

Dear Henriette,

I thank you for giving me a few details of Henri's death. It is horrible! Your vigil next to that poor dead man! It's macabre! It is like those macabre scenes that one finds in the journal of Marie Tarnowska!*

You must have been so frightened! Are you certain that he was really dead? Sometimes heart ailments produce strange effects. He might perhaps have been in a coma! I wouldn't have been convinced in your place! You would be happy if you saw him return! You will never get used to being without him! I think what was harmful to him were the probings they did when he had a retention of urine, generally, probings cause paralysis. I had no idea that he was so ill! His death has affected me deeply, I can't get over it. When I received your announcement, I was in such a fury that I took all my wax models and threw them into the fire, they made a huge blaze and I warmed my feet by the light of the fire, that's what I do when something unpleasant happens to me, I take my hammer and I crush a figure. The death of Henri cost a lot! more than 10,000 francs.

The big statue was quick to follow the fate of its little wax sisters for the death of Henri was followed a few days later with more bad news: without any warning, they all of a sudden stopped giving me any money, I find myself, from one day to the next, without any resources, it is Rodin's band that has worked on Mother's head to obtain this result. And a lot of other capital executions took place right away afterwards, a pile of plaster rubbish is accumulating in the middle of my studio, it's a veritable human sacrifice.

I received a letter from Charles.† Poor cousin! He's always good and generous the way he always was: he invites me to go to Reims. He is always the same, like his mother. Unfortunately, I cannot leave, I refuse

---

*Camille is probably thinking of Marie Bashkirtseff, who was born in the Ukraine in 1860 and as a child emigrated with her mother to France, where she lived in Paris and Nice. She frequented literary and artistic circles, knew Maupassant, Barrès and Bastien-Lepage, and kept a journal from the age of twelve. She died at the age of twenty-four.
†Charles Thierry, Camille Claudel's cousin.

to budge. As soon as I go out, Rodin and his band come into my studio and rob me. All of the Quai Bourbon is infested! Also, now, my studio has been transformed into a fortress: security chains, machicolations, wolf traps behind each door attest to the little confidence that humanity inspires in me. Since I last saw you, I've been beset with all the horrors, sickness, lack of money, badly treated by everyone. Still now, at this very moment, I'm up to my ears in troubles.

As for you, my dear Henriette, I advise you to be careful; what happened to Henri can also happen to you; death which took him away so randomly could do the same to you!

What you tell me about Alfred makes me sad, it is not his fault, he has suffered so much that one mustn't make a crime out of his peculiarities. I send you my affectionate greetings as well as to all your family. As soon as I get out of this mess (supposing I can get out) I will come and see you with great pleasure. It is time for our little reunions, poor Henri, he will no longer be sitting at table with us.

With my sincere affection for you and all your little family,

Your cousin,
K. Momille

Camille Claudel to Henriette Thierry. Early 1913.

My dear Henriette,
I did indeed receive your letter informing me of the death of one of your relatives but since I last saw you, I have had so many troubles that I've lost my head and I couldn't go. At this moment, M. Rodin has persuaded my relatives to have me locked up. They are all in Paris because of that. The scoundrel will then, as a result of this suit, take possession of my life's work. That's how the Protestants and the Jews ruin the Christians, getting them each riled up against the other.

If by chance, you come by here on a walk (in the evening, around eight or nine o'clock), knock against the shutters and I will speak to you but I won't be able to let you in for fear of being suspected of still more horrors!

In any case, I wanted at least one family member to know what is going

136

on. If I manage once again to divert this storm, I will see you afterwards and will explain what it is about.

With all my affectionate greetings,
C. Claudel

Camille Claudel to Henriette Thierry,
from the Montdevergues Asylum.

My dear Henriette,

It is from far away that I write you! It is no longer from my pretty little studio on Quai Bourbon! Since the day I was carried away out the window from my home, I have tried to communicate with you often! Impossible, I am watched at night as well as during the day like a criminal. I don't know whether this letter will reach you! First, I was committed to Ville-Évrard, then, under the pretext of the war, we were taken here to Montdevergues, near Avignon (Vaucluse). Useless to try and describe all what I have suffered since I was torn away from my studio to be locked up in these horrible homes! In the beginning, Charles Thierry tried to get me out but I have had no news since!

Dear Henriette, if you want to write and give me your news and that of your dear children, you would give me enormous pleasure! Don't speak to anyone about this letter for you would only cause me trouble and if you like, answer me at this address:

Mad^e Vv^e Blanc

Tour Philippe le Bel

à Villeneuve-les-Avignon

près Avignon

Vaucluse

This person has been kind enough to offer me her help. Therefore, use a large envelope with the above address and a smaller one inside with my name.

Please accept, dear Henriette, my very affectionate and sincere greetings to you and to your dear children,

Mlle. Camille Claudel
à Montedevergues par Montfavet Vaucluse

137

Louise Claudel to the Mother Superior of the Montdevergues Asylum. January 16, 1915.

Madame Superior,

I am writing you to inquire about the health of my daughter, Mlle. Claudel, a boarder with you since she left Ville-Évrard. I received yesterday, I don't know by what intermediary, two letters from her in which she bitterly complains about the way she was mistreated at Ville-Évrard. She also asks me whether she can leave that establishment for yours.

Are these complaints true? Can you tell me? We have always believed that she was very well looked after. But since she wishes to stay with you, would you be kind enough to let me know how that could be arranged and send me a prospectus?

We cannot leave to go and see her now, the circumstances do not permit it. Since she seems fond of you, we are pleased and encouraged by her good sense.

She says in one of her letters that she is writing a pack of letters everywhere.

I hope you keep those letters because as I have often warned, none of those letters, whoever they may be for, must be mailed to avoid the trouble they caused us, time and again, last year. Except to me and to her brother, M. Paul Claudel, I formally forbid her to write to anyone or to receive any communication, visit or letter from anyone. You could never imagine what happened last year. The director and the doctor in charge were advised of it as well as the head supervisor, Miss Héraud. I cannot tell you the danger of letting her write to who knows whom. I hope that under no pretext has that occurred.

Please accept my apologies, Madame Superior, and my gratitude for the good care with which you surround my daughter; I look forward to your answer when you have the time.

With this letter, I enclose another one for her which I won't seal so that you can read it but please seal it after you have read it.

Louise Claudel

P.S. I particularly bring to the attention of Madame Superior the letters that Mlle. Claudel might write or receive from one named Charles Thierry, her so-called cousin, who is the most infamous scoundrel.

Louise Claudel to the director of the Montdevergues Asylum.
January 26, 1915.

Sir,

Thank you for the letter you wrote me on January 21 in which you assure me that my daughter, Camille Claudel, never had to suffer any ill treatment at the hands of the Ville-Évrard personnel, a fact of which I was fairly certain.

But in her interest and for her well-being, don't you think I should grant what she so urgently requests? Perhaps the new environment in which she lives now and which pleases her, the religious services in which she participates and also the good climate of the south which she enjoys will prove beneficial influences on her mental state? Don't you agree, sir?

We would be pleased to have your opinion on this subject and since you are kind enough to offer to give me the necessary information to make the administrative change, I ask you for it today and hope you will forgive me for troubling you.

Also, we would like to know if my daughter's persecution complex is still as strong as when she was at Ville-Évrard or if there has been an improvement and there is hope for a cure.

Please accept my thanks in advance, sir, for your trouble.

I remain respectfully yours,
L. Claudel

Louise Claudel to the director of the Montdevergues Asylum.
February 10, 1915.

Sir,

This morning I received the answer from the director of Ville-Évrard which I am conveying to you.

I thus ask you to officially enroll Mlle. Claudel, my daughter, subject to the rules of your establishment as of February 10, 1915.

I wish her to be placed in first class and consequently to have a room of her own. As for the payment of her board, which, according to the prospectus, is 5 francs 15 a day, we will abide by the conditions.

I trust that the wardrobe since it was furnished at Ville-Évrard about two years ago has followed our patient or that it will be delivered to you after her arrival.

Since all the papers required for her admission into your establishment were delivered to the administration in the month of March 1913 when she was first admitted, I don't believe it is necessary to furnish them again?

We, my son and I, are at your disposal in the event that you should want us to meet with other conditions.

I hope that this change of residence and environment will prove beneficial for my daughter, it is she who asked us for it, we are confident that we will congratulate ourselves for the decision we made today.

I remain respectfully yours,
L. Claudel

Louise Claudel to the director of the Montdevergues Asylum.
February 15, 1915.

Sir,

I received your letter advising me of the enrollment of my daughter, Mlle. Claudel, under the rules of your establishment and I thank you for your diligence in rendering us this service.

I hope it will be for her own good and that she will continue to be happy with you, in the company of the good sisters whom she seems to like very much. I would like to receive news of her from time to time, for example, every fifteen days. But at least every month.

I insist that she not send any letters to anyone nor that she receive any, except for mine and those from her brother, Paul Claudel, and that she be unable to slip letters on the sly.

The troubles we had on account of this which you well know force me to impose this condition.

Likewise, I ask you not to send any medical reports unless you advise us first to whom.

I will forward the sum of 300 francs today to the cashier to be put into our account.

Respectfully yours,
L. Claudel

Maria Paillette to Camille Claudel. March 12, 1915.

My dear Camille,

I am a bit late answering your New Year's letter. Don't be angry with me. We've had a terrible time here at home. On the 20th of February, in the evening (nearly a month already), someone knocks at the street door; it's the local policeman who is all upset and starts to stammer. He didn't have to say a word. Mother understood right away. My little brother was killed. I can't bring myself to believe it. How sad this war is! How long will it last? But don't worry, Camille, I won't forget you. Your letter from Montdevergues made me very sad. How can one be so mean as to keep you locked up when you haven't done anything? After all, it's not a crime to want to live alone and to like cats. If so, half the village would be locked up! Your mother, whom I met Monday at the bakery, told me that they would take you out as soon as the war is over. Why not right away? I don't understand. I think of you often. Do you know that I still have the beautiful picture you did of me at my dressing table in my room? Unfortunately, it is not framed . . .

I send you a kiss, your friend,
Maria

Camille Claudel to her cousin.[*] *Around 1915.*

My dear cousin,

Despite the different adventures that have kept us apart, I haven't forgotten that next Thursday is Sainte Marie-Madeleine and I want to celebrate your feast day as if I were still near you.

Unfortunately, it is not with flower in hand that I come offering you my wishes but with tears in my eyes. The tears of exile, the tears I have shed drop by drop since I was torn away from my dear studio. You who understand how attached I am to my art must know what I had to suffer when I was suddenly separated from my precious work, you who know me so well in spite of my foolishness and my inconsistencies!

My poor cousin!

The oak tree in Villeneuve no longer exists, I am not the only one aware

---

[*] The cousin referred to is unknown.

of it, also I don't want to sadden you further with a recital of the injustices I have fallen victim to.

I hardly dare ask for your news! Trembling, I ask myself if you are still alive, if you haven't disappeared in this horrible war that devastates our beautiful country. If you want to write me a word, you would make me very happy. By a singular act of fate, I now find myself a boarder at Montde-vergues near Montfavet (Vaucluse) in an establishment run by the Sisters of Saint-Charles.

As you are an intrepid traveler, if by chance one day you find yourself near here, don't forget your little sculptor cousin (the one who was always losing her umbrella).

> I pray the dear Lord for you and your sisters.
> Camille

Camille Claudel to Paul Claudel. After May 1915.

My dear Paul,
I wrote to Mother several times, in Paris, in Villeneuve, without getting a word in reply.

You yourself came to see me at the end of May and I made you promise to look after me and not leave me abandoned like this.

How is it that you haven't written me a single time since and that you haven't returned to see me. Do you think I enjoy spending months like this, the years without ever any news, without a hope!

What is the reason for this cruelty? How do they manage to lead you so astray? I would like to know.

I wrote to Mother asking her to transfer me to Sainte-Anne in Paris which would give me the advantage of being closer to all of you and the opportunity to explain clearly the different points that still need to be cleared up. In addition, it would be an opportunity for you to economize since one can stay at Sainte-Anne for 90 francs a month. I am not suggesting that at that price it will be like paradise, far from it, but since I left my studio on Quai Bourbon, I am accustomed to everything. Should they send me to Siberia, nothing would astonish me.

To tell the truth, I would prefer to return to ordinary life and forget all these adventures.

You can tell Mother that if she is afraid that I will claim the Villeneuve property, I have no such intention; I would rather make a gift to Jacques of everything I inherit and spend the rest of my life in peace.

I would even prefer to be only a maid than to continue to live like this. Have you looked after my things that you told me you stored in Villeneuve? Have you made sure that they haven't fallen into the hands of the friends of that scoundrel who dealt me this pretty blow so that he could take them? He is scared silly to see me return before he has had time to get his hands on . . .

That is why he keeps delaying my getting out for as long as possible; he is trying to gain time and in the interval, all sorts of things are going to happen that you don't expect. You will be punished for your apathy; so beware.

I am waiting for a letter from you soon.

> My love to your wife and to your children.
> C.C.

Louise Claudel to the director of the Montdevergues Asylum. September 11, 1915.

Sir,

Please excuse me for using you as an intermediary in order that my daughter, C. Claudel, a boarder in your establishment, can receive a letter in answer to hers in which she asked me to take her back instantly to live with me.

That is not possible. I am very old and at no cost can I give in to her demand. I would have no authority over her and I would have to suffer all her whims. Never will I consent to this arrangement. She has pulled the wool over our eyes for too long.

She is fine with you, she was happy enough there awhile ago. How is it that she no longer wants to stay? She complains about the food and also that her letters are not mailed to her friends who would come to save her if they knew how unhappy she was. Someone told her, and they were quite wrong to do so, that it was by my order that she received no news from anyone, it was pointless to tell her that, it would only provoke her.

I am writing you these things, sir, so as to keep you abreast of what kind of relations we have with her and to ask for your support in making her understand that she must stay with you.

She asks me to send her some money to have her teeth fixed. I don't ask for anything better but what sum must I forward to her?

Respectfully yours,
L. Claudel

Louise Claudel to the director of the Montdevergues Asylum. October 20, 1915.

Sir,

Yesterday I received another letter from my daughter, C. Claudel, in which she informed me that she was very unhappy and wished to be transferred to Sainte-Anne in Paris. I am very anxious to know how she manages to send me letters by means other than through the doctor and yourself. I am extremely worried for she could just as easily write to others who would use the letters to continue the campaign which they began two years ago against us.

At no cost do I want to remove her from your establishment where she was content not too long ago. I will not have her changing establishments every six months and as far as taking her back with me or sending her back home like she was, never, never. I am 75 years old, I cannot take care of a daughter who has the most absurd ideas, who wishes us ill, who hates us and is ready to do us all the evil she can. If one has to pay an additional sum for her board so that she will be more comfortable, I don't ask for anything better, but keep her, I beg you.

At home, she lived like a destitute person, she hadn't seen a single soul in the past 10 years, she was robbed by everyone who sold food to her. The doors and windows were chained, padlocked, and whatever she ate was put in a packing case on top of one of the windows. As for her person and her apartment, it was something horrible. She spent her time writing

144

letters to good-for-nothings and making denunciations.

In short, she has all the vices, I don't want to see her again, she has done us too much harm. Again, I beg you, sir, to find out by whom she sends the letters and to forbid her to write by any other means than that of the administration.

Respectfully yours,
L. Claudel

Camille Claudel to Mlle. Gésuà. Around 1915.

Dear Mlle. Gésuà,

It is with great sadness that we have just learned about the death of your poor mother! . . . She was indeed quickly snatched from your affection, you hardly had the time to see her again and she was taken away from you!

You certainly have been sorely tried, dear Mlle. Gésuà!

Above all, don't let your imagination get the better of you, stay very calm so that no new misfortunes can befall you!

To tell you the truth, this death concerns me especially, as I am always afraid that the same thing will happen to my mother! I live in mortal fear just thinking of everything that can happen at home while I am locked up here! What a misfortune should Mother die while I was here not able to move! What a worry for me! because Mother does not admit it but she is not happy! . . . When I think that my poor father was already dead without my knowing a thing about it and that he asked to see his daughter, his daughter! and his daughter never came! Mother wrote me a letter a few days ago but she does not speak at all about taking me out, there is still no question of my leaving! I have cried a lot since you left. When you were here, it gave me a bit of courage! I am the one who has taken your place in chapel but I am a long way from having your fine presence!

I have to go to Avignon tomorrow with Sister Saint Hildefonse to have my teeth fixed.

The sisters are very sympathetic to your misfortune as are all the people who knew you!

Dear Mlle. Gésuà! Nevertheless think of your unfortunate companion of Montdevergues! I would have asked you to go see my mother but she is not in Paris, she is in Villeneuve-sur-Fère in Tardenois, Aisne.

Remember me to your brothers and sisters,
C.C.

Louise Claudel to the director of the Montdevergues Asylum.
August 8, 1918.

Sir,

I have had no news of my daughter, Camille Claudel, your boarder, since the beginning of the month of May.

As our region (Villeneuve-sur-Fère in the Tardenois) was taken and has been occupied by the Germans for the last three months, I had to seek refuge here and I await the outcome of events before returning to Paris for I cannot think of returning to Villeneuve.

Thus, I ask that you send my daughter's health bulletins here and all other information that concerns her.

Respectfully yours,
Widow Claudel, at Belmont (Ain) care of Mme. Nicolas

Louise Claudel to the director of the Montdevergues Asylum.
March 9, 1919.

Sir,

I am taking the liberty of bringing to your attention the complaints I have received from my daughter, Camille Claudel, whom you recently returned to third class.

She urgently wishes that you have her trunk put in her room so that she won't have to climb the stairs.

Also, she asks that she be advised when a package arrives for her so that it won't lie about for days or that it be brought up to her room.

Sir, I don't want to insist any further. I entrust my poor daughter to

146

your kindness, subject to your rules, and I am very grateful to you. She desires to have an alcohol lamp as well but probably you won't permit it.

> With my thanks, sir, I remain respectfully yours,
> Widow Claudel

Louise Claudel to the director of the Montdevergues Asylum. September 6, 1919.

Sir,

I am taking the liberty of sending you the enclosed letter[*] which I am sending to my daughter Camille Claudel.

It is an answer to her letter in which she accuses us of a lot of things to which we are strangers, that is why my letter is so harsh.

Her state of mind is always the same, always believing herself to be the victim of everything which is not in the slightest bit true. It is she who has been her own executioner.

I apologize, sir, for making use of you as an intermediary but since I know that the rule forbids writing to the person directly, I thought it possible to ask you to give my daughter the letter today after you have sealed it.

> With my thanks, sir, I remain respectfully yours,
> Widow Claudel

Louise Claudel to Camille Claudel. September 1919.

Dear daughter,

Your last letter is before my eyes and I can't imagine that you can write such horrors to your mother. God alone knows what I will have suffered on account of my children! Paul blames me because, according to him, we favored Louise to his detriment and you, Camille, how dare you accuse me of poisoning your father! You know as well as I do that he was nearly 90 years old when he left us, that I did all that was in my power to keep him alive as long as possible for you. How terribly he suffered, too, when

[*] The letter said to be enclosed follows.

147

he learned the truth about your relations with Rodin and the disgraceful comedy you performed for us. And I, I was naïve enough to invite the "Great Man" to Villeneuve with Mme. Rodin, his concubine! While you, you played the sweet innocent and were living with him as a kept woman. I hardly dare write the words that come to mind. According to you, we, Louise and I, are under the thumb of Berthelot, Paul's friend. You say "he pulls the strings," it is your expression. When one thinks of Berthelot's kindness to us, one has to be dreaming; that's not all. Louise, you claim, stole your inheritance? The poor child who had so much trouble raising Jacques, to find him a position . . . Let's stop here, shall we? Your letter is nothing but a mass of slanders, each more odious than the next. But you don't tell me if you received the coat I sent you from La Samaritaine or if Félix Potin did, in fact, send off the coffee and the tea biscuits that you asked for. Naturally, that does not count.

I send you a kiss.

Johany Peytel, president of the Crédit Algérien, to the director of the Montdevergues Asylum. September 1, 1920.

Sir,

Mlle. Claudel, who was a distinguished artist, is confined in your asylum. I admired the courageous way of life and the artistic talent of this unfortunate woman. My wife and I have always felt a profound sympathy for her. I take the liberty of addressing her the enclosed letter in which I have included a 100 franc note. I would be very grateful if you could give it to her or, in any case, make use of it to improve her pitiful condition: perhaps, too, she will feel herself less abandoned.

With my thanks, sir, and best regards.

Louise Claudel to the director of the Montdevergues Asylum. June 1920.

Sir,

Yesterday, I received the health bulletin on my daughter, Camille Claudel, a boarder in your establishment. You tell me that her persecution complex has diminished and one could let her out on a trial basis. This, sir, is the subject I wish to discuss with you.

148

According to the letters that I receive from her, I see that her ideas have not changed. She continues to treat us like thieves who turned over to her enemies her studio filled with works of art and accuses us of having thrown into the dump all her boxes which, among other things, contained a monument of Victor Hugo, a group of *Gossipers,* etc., while in fact the cases were filled with nothing more than packages of shapeless clay which we had a lot of trouble getting rid of. It is impossible to believe that she has a healthy mind and that she can behave reasonably, no more so now than when she first entered the home for mental patients in which, no longer able to cope with her incoherencies, we had to place her.

If she were to leave you, she would begin again immediately, I am certain, and would cause us the biggest problems.

One cannot allow those who suffer from a persecution complex freedom without grave danger because once back in their own surroundings, they quickly resume their old ideas.

I don't live at home but with my second daughter; I am very old, often sick, thus, I cannot have her who is with you, nor can I authorize you to let her out on a trial basis. I cannot make such a decision without consulting my son who is in Copenhagen. At his earliest visit, we will speak of it and reach a decision which I will impart to you.

Respectfully yours,
Widow Claudel

Louise Claudel to the director of the Montdevergues Asylum.
July 9, 1920.

Sir,

In your last health bulletin on my daughter, Mlle. Claudel, you advise me to remove her from your establishment and place her in one closer to Paris.

I don't ask for anything better but I must have time to think about it before carrying out this project.

I don't know of any homes that take in boarders at the price of yours and I don't know how to find out about them.

My resources are limited to the sum that I now pay for her, impossible for me to give more. You know that on account of the war, I lost nearly everything I owned and that I must wait a few years for the war damages promised to me as well as those from the Russian front. Nor can I allow her to be completely free, for according to her letters, her ideas have not changed, she continues to accuse people willy-nilly of all sorts of misdeeds. She would lead the same life all over again the way she did before 1913. In Ville-Évrard, one saw in what a state we found her. One of our best friends, Abbé Martin, is willing to pay you a visit at the beginning of August, around the 6th. He will see you as well as my daughter. He will speak with her and you can discuss with him what we might do. We trust him implicitly and it will be as if we were talking to you. I am counting a great deal on this interview so as to arrange matters and make a decision. I would venture that she is not completely cured and that it is necessary to keep her under surveillance for a while longer.

Respectfully yours,
Widow Claudel

*Louise Claudel to the director of the Montdevergues Asylum.
October 17, 1920.*

Sir,
I have just received the notice concerning the increase in boarding fees at your establishment.

As you know, my daughter, Camille Claudel, because of the persecution complex from which she suffers, does not benefit from the food given to those in second class where she is and she eats only baked potatoes, eggs and very little other food. Consequently, couldn't I obtain a special price for her in accordance with her expenses! I hope you will examine my request, sir, and take it into consideration as well as be favorably disposed toward it.

While I await your reply, sir, I remain respectfully yours,
Widow Claudel

*Louise Claudel to the director of the Montdevergues Asylum.
April 4, 1924.*

Sir,
I am writing in regard to my daughter, Camille Claudel, a boarder in your establishment. There is a question, says she, of moving her from her room

150

to the second floor where she would have only one room—a much smaller one with no furniture in which to put away her things.

If, in fact, you have such a plan, I beg you, sir, not to do anything and to leave her in the room she has occupied for so long.

It would make us very unhappy to see her housed in such cramped quarters against her will. If you must ask us to pay additional board to grant us this favor, please let us know and we shall comply. My son, who will be returning to France shortly, would be very upset to see his sister so uncomfortably lodged when he goes to see her.

Please grant us this favor and rest assured that I am very much obliged to you. I am very put out not to be able to go and see her but, at my age, I cannot consider undertaking such a journey. I wait for events to lend themselves to a reconciliation and in the meantime, I entrust her to your good will.

> Respectfully yours,
> Widow Claudel

Louise Claudel to the director of the Montdevergues Asylum. November 18, 1926.

Sir,

I am replying to your letter dated October 26 in which you ask if I accept the increase of boarding fees required by the general council of the Vaucluse.

I accept it and I don't want to change anything in my daughter's position in your establishment, all the same I am sorry not to be able to move her to a higher class.

She is in third class, I adhere to everything that she has been granted thus far and I entrust her to your good will.

> Respectfully yours,
> Widow Claudel

Camille Claudel to Louise Claudel. February 2, 1927.

My dear Mother,

I am very late writing you because it has been so cold that I could barely stand up. To write I could not bring myself to go to the common room where a mean little fire burns, the racket there is infernal. I am forced to stay put in my room on the second floor where it is so icy that I am numb, my fingers shake and I can't hold a pen.

I haven't been warm all winter. I am frozen to the bone and bent in two by the cold. I had a very bad cold. One of my friends, a poor teacher from the Lycée Fénélon who ended up here, was found dead from cold in her bed. It is terrible. You have no idea of how cold it is in Montdevergues. And it lasts seven months in all. Never can you know how much I suffer in these homes. Also to my surprise and horror, I learned that Paul was going to have me put in first class. Strange how you have never been here yet you know better than I what suits me. You spend money left and right: who knows all that you have spent?

I have already told you several times that those in first class are the most miserable. First of all, their dining room is in a draft, they sit at a tiny little table, all squeezed together. From one end of the year to the other, they all have dysentery, not a sign that the food is good. The basic food is as follows. Soup, that is to say, water and badly cooked vegetables without ever any meat. An old beef stew in an oily black sauce, sour all the year round, an old dish of macaroni swimming in grease, or an old dish of rice of the same sort, in one word, just plain grease, for hors d'oeuvres, a few tiny [illegible word] of raw ham, for dessert, some stringy old dates, three tough old figs or three old biscuits or an old piece of she-goat cheese. So much for your 20 francs a day. The wine is vinegar, the coffee is chick-pea water. That's the real proof of madness to spend money like that. As for the room, it's the same thing, there is nothing in it at all, not a quilt or a sanitary bucket, nothing, an ugly chipped chamber pot only three quarters of the time, an ugly iron bed on which one shakes with cold all night long (I who hate iron beds, you should see how I suffer in it, so consequently, I beg you to act according to my taste and not yours). I don't want to stay in first class at any price and when you receive this letter, I beg you to have me put back in third where I was before. In spite of my pleas, since you stubbornly insist on keeping me in mental homes where I am horribly unhappy and denied any kind of justice, at least economize your money and if it's Paul, let him know my opinions.

Do you have any news of him? Do you know where he is now? What are his plans in regard to me? Does he intend to let me die in lunatic asylums? You are very harsh to refuse me a shelter in Villeneuve. I won't make trouble like you think. I would be too happy to resume ordinary life to do anything at all. I wouldn't dare move, so much have I suffered. You say someone would have to take care of me? How so? I've never had a maid in my life, you are the one who always needed one.

Were you to give me the old Regnier woman's room and the kitchen, you could shut the rest of the house. I would do absolutely nothing reprehensible, I have suffered too much ever to get over it.

Don't you see that they are lying to you on purpose to always take your money.

I received the hat, it fits, the coat is fine, the stockings, they are wonderful, and the rest of what you sent me.

> I send you a kiss,
> Camille.

Send me your news right away and tell if you got the flu.

I have received your letter which reassures me because knowing that they were going to change my class, I assumed you were dead, so I didn't sleep at night, I froze. Above all, don't think of sending more money after the letter I just wrote you, either for firewood or anything else, your money goes straight to the office, period, that's all, while I, I must suffer like a martyr. Don't do anything without consulting me first. Lunatic asylums are specifically designed to make people suffer, one can't do anything about it especially if one never sees anyone. Mainly, hurry and write Paul to have me put back the way I was before, for I could still eat and in first class, I won't be able to eat at all. I don't want to go near all that fat which makes me terribly sick, I've asked for baked potatoes noon and night, I'll live off them, is it worth paying 20 francs for that? Proof that you are the ones who are crazy. As for me, I am so heartbroken that I have to keep living here that I am no longer a human being. I can't stand the screams of all those creatures anymore, they break my heart. God, how I wish I were back in Villeneuve!

I didn't do what I did to end up as a large number in a mental home. I deserved something else, may it please Berthelot.

You ask me what I need in my next package. Don't put any chocolate as I still have a lot.

Put 1 kilo of Brazilian coffee (it is excellent)
1 kilo of butter
1 kilo of sugar and more
1 kilo of flour
½ pound of tea, always the same
2 bottles of wine (white)
½ bottle of ordinary oil
1 little parcel of salt
1 piece of soap
2 boxes of cubes (I still have some)
a few mandarins, if you can, put in a little jar of brandied cherries, but
   if it is too expensive, don't put any in.

That will be enough like that.

> I send you a kiss,
> Camille

Louise Claudel to the director of the Montdevergues Asylum.
February 6, 1927.

Sir,
You have received a letter from my son, M. Claudel, in which he asked
you to put his sister, C. Claudel, in 1st class and to provide her with
every possible comfort. I am writing to ask you to wait for another letter
from M. Claudel before you act on this request and to leave my daughter in 3rd class in the room she had. She is happier there than in 1st; I
want to satisfy her. Therefore, I ask you to keep the advance of 3,000
francs that you have received and not to change anything in her way of
life.

   She wants it done instantly.

   Only give her what she wants out of this sum and she should ask you
for it herself.

> Respectfully yours,
> Widow Claudel

Camille Claudel to Louise Claudel. February 18, 1927.

Dear Mother,

I received your wonderful package today. It arrived in good shape, all the things are excellent, I am always well fed despite being so far away. The store, Potin, is most conscientious, you can compliment them; the wine is delicious and does me a world of good, the coffee is delicious, the butter too; what a difference compared to the filthy food of lunatic asylums.

I can live again when your package arrives, as a matter of fact, I only live off what it contains, as far as the food is concerned, it makes me horribly sick, it is not at all worth paying 30 francs a day for first.

I ask that you keep this picture for me. I lose everything. It is of a young woman who spent four years here for a nervous breakdown. She has just died. She went back home but she must have died. She must have died from perhaps some kind of a flu. I was a friend of hers. She had gone to boarding school at Épinal with Marie Merklen, Marie's daughter. She wanted to come and see me in Villeneuve and in Paris, she was very rich but she had a lot of trouble getting married, she had lost her whole family except for her father, the Count of B., but since you wouldn't let me leave here, we lost track of each other, I learned of her death age 37. Tell me especially about the details of the wedding.

I send you a kiss and thank you most warmly for the wonderful present.

My regards to Louise and Jacques.
Camille

Camille Claudel to Paul Claudel. March 3, 1927.

My dear Paul,

Not long ago, I had news of you indirectly, I learned that you sent a certain sum of money to the director to improve my lot in so far as that is possible. You are right to trust the director for he is a man who has a great reputation for honesty and who, at the same time, is very kind to me. You can be sure that under the circumstances, he will do everything he can for me while you, I am sure you mean to help me, you certainly make enormous sacrifices for my sake, which in your case are all the more meritorious since you have huge responsibilities everywhere. Five children and nothing but expenses, nothing but trips, nothing but hotels to pay.

I have often asked myself how you manage it all. You must have a very level head to handle everything with so much intelligence, to understand it all, to overcome all the difficulties! I, for one, would never be capable of such a thing!

You mean well and so does the director but in a lunatic asylum these things are very difficult to obtain, changes are difficult to make; even if one wants to, it is difficult to create a state in which things are bearable. There are established rules, there is an adapted way of life, to go against the practices is extremely hard! It means taking into account all sorts of terrible, violent, yelling, threatening creatures. One needs a very strict discipline for that, occasionally even a harsh one, otherwise one would never see the end of it. It all screams, sings, yells at the top of its lungs from morning to night and night to morning. These are creatures whose own parents can't abide them, they are so terrible and noxious. And how is it that I should be forced to stand them? To say nothing of the troubles that arise from such promiscuity? It laughs, it sobs, it tells stories that never end where the details get all jumbled up and lost! How awful to be in the middle of it all, I have to be taken out of this place after fourteen years today that I was committed! I shout out loud for freedom. My dream would be to return to Villeneuve right away and never again move, I would rather have an old barn in Villeneuve than to be a first-class boarder here. Those in first are no better off than the ones in third. It is exactly the same thing especially for me who lives off my own diet; useless then to increase the cost on that score. The money you sent could be used to pay for third class. It is not without regret that I watch you spend your money on a lunatic asylum. Money which I could use to make beautiful works and to live comfortably! What a misfortune! I could weep about it. Arrange with the director to have me returned to third class or else take me out of here right away, that would be even better. What happiness if I could find myself back again at Villeneuve! That lovely Villeneuve, there's nothing quite like it on earth! It was fourteen years ago today that I had the unpleasant surprise of seeing two policemen enter my studio, they were armed to the teeth, helmeted and booted, and very menacing. Sad surprise for an artist: instead of a reward, this is what happened to me! I am the one these things happen to, I've always been the butt of meanness. God, what I have had to endure since that day. And no hope it will ever end. Each time I write to Mother to take me back to Villeneuve, she answers that the house is about to cave in. It is for the best from all points of view. Nevertheless, I am longing to leave this place. The longer it is, the harder it is! New boarders arrive all the time, one on top of the other, *foussi* as we we say in Villeneuve, enough to believe that the whole world is going mad.

I don't know if you intend to leave me here but it is very cruel of you! They tell me that you are coming back for the wedding of your daughter on April 20. It is very likely that you won't have time to think of me; they'll arrange to send you to foreign countries for meetings again. They'll know how to drive you far away from Paris and from me, especially, I'll have little chance to reach you. The only thing I want is to leave here, no modification can ever make me happy here; there is no possible good in it. We have had a terrible winter; the wind never stopped blowing for six months, the icy Arctic Ocean is nothing compared to this!

To know that one is so comfortable in Paris and to have to give it up for a few whims in your head.

I have heard it said that Reine has been very sick and that she had to undergo a painful operation. Let's hope that she is better now. It seems that Louise, too, was fairly sick, all of which makes me tremble. Above all, should a misfortune occur, don't abandon me here all alone and don't do anything without consulting me. Considering that I know the customs of the establishment, I am the one who knows what I need.

Luckily, I have the support of Doctor Charponel and that of the director. I thank you for writing them. Don't take offense at my letter. If you don't intend to come and see me, you should convince Mother to make the trip, I would be happy to see her again. With the express train, it is not as tiring as one says; she could easily do that for me in spite of her advanced age.

With that, I leave you and send you a kiss and also one to your daughter Gigette, who I believe is still with you.

Your wife did not want to see me, nor did the others. I no longer hope to see them again.

Your sister Camille

Camille Claudel to Paul Claudel. March 3, 1930.

Dear Paul,

Today, the 3rd of March, is the anniversary of the day I was taken to Ville-Évrard: that makes 17 years since Rodin and the art dealers sent me away to lunatic asylums to do penance. After they got hold of all my life's work and used Rodin to do their dirty deed, they have condemned me to years in prison which they themselves would have soundly deserved. Rodin was but an agent whom they used to impress you and to employ you to do the job which worked out just as they planned, thanks to your credulity and to Mother's and Louise's. Don't forget that Rodin's wife was an old model of his: now do you see the scheme of which I was the object? It's nice, all these millionaires who attack a poor defenseless artist! Because all the gentlemen who collaborated on this pretty affair are all more than forty times millionaires. It seems that my poor studio, some bits of shabby furniture, some tools I carved myself, my poor household goods still aroused their greed! Since the imagination, emotion, the new, the unexpected, are part of a fine mind and unknown to them, the block-heads, thick brains forever shut to the light, they need someone to furnish it for them. They used to say: "We use a dreamer to find us our subject matter."

There should be someone at least who would be truly grateful and know how to give some compensation to the poor woman whom they robbed of her genius: no! a lunatic asylum! not even the right to have her own home! . . . Because I have to remain at their mercy! That is exploiting women, crushing the artist who is made to sweat blood! It appears that the principal beneficiary of my studio is M. Hébrardt, art editor of the rue Royale. That's where all my sketches (more than 500) disappeared. It seems that already a few years before I left Paris, the sketches I did at Villeneuve all ended up with him (by what miracle? God alone knows). I found some of them again at his place, they were produced in bronze and signed by other artists: it's really too much! . . . And to condemn me to perpetual prison so that I won't complain! All of that actually comes straight out of Rodin's diabolical brain. He had only one idea, that he being dead, I would come into my own as an artist and be better than he. He had to keep me in his clutches after his death as he did during his life.

158

Whether he was dead or alive, I had to be unhappy. He has succeeded on all counts, for unhappy I am! That must not bother you very much, but I am!

From time to time, they pretend to improve my lot but it doesn't last long, it's a sham! Lately, they have built a big kitchen about 1 kilometer away from the home; that provided me with an outing and a walk. It didn't last . . . I got the order not to go there anymore, without a reason, again I've been confined.

I am so weary of this bondage. I would so love to be at home and able to shut the door properly. I don't know if this dream will come true, to be home. I received a letter from Jessie Elborne recently. She says that she is coming here with her husband toward the end of April! They are very kind but what can they do for me!

I think they have enough troubles of their own.

In all the family, there isn't anyone who does as much.

I have no news of your children.

My greetings to you and your family.

Camille Claudel to Paul Claudel. April 4, 1932.

My dear Paul,

Yesterday, Saturday, I had a lovely surprise, they called me down to the sitting room and there were Chouchette, Roger and Pierre.* One could not have given me a nicer surprise. Chouchette was very pretty, very well dressed. Pierre has grown a lot, he looks exactly like you. Roger was very kind to me, right away he set about seeing to food, he went to Montfavet and brought me back oranges, some bananas, butter, croissants, apples and he gave me a bit of money. He did all these errands without batting an eye, he seemed very capable to me. I received them hobbledy-hop with rheumatism on my knee, wearing a worn-out old coat, an old hat from the Samaritaine which fell down on my nose. Anyway, it was me. Pierre remembered his crazy old aunt. That's how I'll appear when they remember me in the next century.

He told me you would come soon.

I am waiting for you.

---

*Roger Méquillier was Marie (Chouchette) Claudel's husband and Pierre Claudel was the elder son of Paul Claudel.

I am going through a bad period at the moment. They've begun installing the central heating. There are workmen all over the house, scaffolding all over the courtyard. Oh, God, it's so tedious, I would so like to be next to the fireplace in Villeneuve but alas! I don't think I'll ever leave Montdevergues, the way things are moving! It does not look good!

I am very worried about what is happening in the Far East. Between Japan and China, who knows what will happen next?

I am afraid that you will be mixed up in all that, I am very worried. I haven't been back to Avignon because of my rheumatism, I can't move.

I send you a kiss with all my heart and with my thanks, I see that you haven't completely abandoned me.

Pierre has a kind look about him.

My best to Reine, Henri, Gigette and Renée (the whole band).[*]

Draft of a letter from Camille Claudel to Paul Claudel, unfinished and undated. Around 1932.

My dear Paul,

I have to hide to write you and I don't know how I'll get my letter mailed. The woman on duty who usually grants me this favor (in return for greasing her palm!) is sick. The others would betray me to the director like a criminal. For don't forget, Paul, your sister is in prison. In prison and with lunatics who yell all day long, make faces, are incapable of saying three words that make sense. For nearly twenty years, that is the treatment inflicted on an innocent; as long as Mother was alive, I never stopped begging her to get me out of here, to put me somewhere else, anywhere, in a hospital, in a convent, but not with lunatics. Each time, I ran up against a wall. In Villeneuve, it seems, it was impossible. Why? I've said it a thousand times. One would have had to hire a servant to look after me!! As if I were senile, it sends shivers up and down my spine. I was counting on you but unhappily I see now that you have always let yourself be manipulated by Berthelot and his clique. They only had one thing in mind, those people: that I leave Paris so that they could grab my work, make themselves rich without any trouble. And right behind them, Rodin with his tart. I have

---

[*] Henri, Gigette and Renée were Paul Claudel's children.

to admit that everything was well worked out and you, poor naïve man, they set you up in their game without your even noticing it. You and Louise and Mother and Father. All of you. As for me, they treated me like a victim of the plague. They spied on me, they sent people to steal my work, I've already told you several times, they tried to poison me. You tell me, God has mercy on the afflicted, God is good, etc. . . . etc. . . . Let's talk about your God who lets an innocent woman rot away in an asylum. I don't know what keeps me from . . .

Eugène Blot to Camille Claudel. September 3, 1932.

Dear Camille,

While filing away papers last month, I found several of your letters to me. I reread them; they all date from 1905, the year I organized your exhibition in my gallery that enthused the critics without, alas, warming the public. So many things have happened since! Your departure, the war, the death of Rodin, the illness that kept me far from Paris until 1926 . . .

I had lost track of you . . . In the wheeler-dealer world of sculpture, Rodin, you, perhaps three or four others had brought authenticity, one does not forget that. X. still has a wonderful memory of your *Beseecher* in marble (which I cast in bronze for the salon of 1904) and considers it to be the manifesto of modern sculpture. At last you were "yourself," totally free of Rodin's influence, your imagination was as great as your craft. Embellished with your signature, the first cast is one of the best pieces in my gallery. I never look at it without a rush of unspeakable emotion. I feel I see you again. Those half-open lips, those quivering nostrils, the light in the gaze, all of which speaks of life and its most essential mystery. With you, one left the world of false appearances for one of thought. What genius! The word is not too strong. How could you have deprived us of so much beauty?

One day, when Rodin was paying me a visit, I saw him suddenly stop in front of this portrait, look at it, gently touch the metal and cry. Yes, cry. Like a child. Fifteen years now since he died. In truth, he never loved anyone but you, Camille, I can say so today. All the rest—miserable adventures, that ridiculous social life, while deep down, he remained a man of the people—it was an outlet for an excessive nature. Oh! I know very well, Camille, that he left you, I am not trying to justify his conduct. You have suffered too much on account of him. But I won't retract what I've just written. Time will put things right. What can I do for you now, dear Camille Claudel? Write me, take the hand I hold out to you. I have never ceased being your friend.

With my affection and respect,
Yours, Eugène Blot

Camille Claudel to Paul Claudel. Undated, probably written in 1938 or 1939 due to the mention of the death of Jacques de Massary, who died in 1938.

My dear Paul,
Yesterday, Saturday, I did indeed receive the fifty francs you kindly sent me and which, I assure you, will certainly be useful (the bursar has not yet paid me back the fifty francs he owes me although I've had the voucher for more than a month). You see how many difficulties there are in this asylum, and who knows if it won't get worse in a little while.

I am very upset to learn that you are still unwell, let us hope that it will be better bit by bit. I am waiting for the visit you promised me next summer but I don't hope for it; Paris is far away and God knows what may happen by then?

Actually, they are trying to force me to sculpt here and seeing that they can't, they are making all sorts of trouble for me but that won't convince me, on the contrary.

At this holiday time, I always think about our dear mother. I never saw her again since the day you took the fateful decision to send me to lunatic asylums! I am thinking about the beautiful portrait I did of her in the shade of our beautiful garden. Her large eyes in which one could read a secret sadness, the spirit of resignation over her whole face, her hands crossed on her knees in total abnegation: all of it suggesting a modesty, a sense of duty pushed to the extreme, that's how she was, our poor mother. I never saw the portrait again (no more than I did her). If you ever hear speak of it, let me know.

---

* This letter appears in Paul Claudel's *Journal II*, page 1005.

162

I doubt whether that odious person about whom I often speak to you has the audacity to attribute it to himself, like my other works, that would be too much, the portrait of my mother!

You won't forget to give me news of Marion?[*]

Tell me also how is Cécile?[†] Is she able to overcome her grief? I don't dare say anymore for fear of always harping on the same thing!

My greetings to you and your family.

Your sister in spirit,
Camille

---

[*] The wife of Pierre Claudel, Paul Claudel's elder son.
[†] Daughter-in-law of Louise Claudel-Massary.

Chapter 7

The Gold She Finds

I don't understand a thing about theoretical questions in matters concerning Art.

Camille Claudel

What strikes one in the work of Camille Claudel is its incompleteness. Perhaps this is what makes it so moving—like the ghost of a beautiful gesture, a feeling prematurely broken off. All of her art is stamped with this quality of absence which must have been a profoundly embedded characteristic of her soul. Although not very perceptive, Rodin was aware of it and it is not by chance that the most beautiful portrait of her he left us, *Thought* (*La Pensée*), presents a face with a vacant gaze being slowly swallowed by indetermination. And it is precisely this quality, as well as the limited number of works—a narrow field of vision for criticism—which renders analysis and aesthetic commentary so difficult.

From the *Young Roman* (*Jeune romain*) to *Maturity* one can follow the progress of an earned autonomy, of an organized thought process, but the masterpiece of maturity is missing—that which, once originality has been established, allows one to find retroactively the precursory signs. (Who could guess the real qualities of a Raphael had he not distanced himself from Perugino, or of a Van Dyck had he died before he took leave of Rubens?) Like all great disciples capable of becoming great masters, the

164

signs of independence in Camille Claudel are closely linked with those of resemblance and are manifestations of admiration and allegiance—the reason why one has always been satisfied to classify her with Rodin's talented students, a historically inexact classification since, properly speaking, Rodin never had any pupils.

Aside from the fact that there was never a school of Rodin, one should not forget Paul Dubois's remark, "It's a Rodin!" when he saw Camille's work prior to the two artists' meeting, or Roger Marx's reminiscences as reported by the Goncourts: "Rodin and the sculptor Claudel worked lovingly together as must have Prud'hon and Mlle. Mayer."[*] And witnesses assure us: Camille Claudel was much more than just a student. If one quotes Rodin himself—"I showed her where she would find gold, but the gold she finds truly belongs to her"—isn't that proof that everyone was well aware that Camille's sculpture was not Rodin's?

Let us try to define this evanescent gold.

One could paint a portrait of a young artist, stubborn and obsessed with her vocation, paint the background gray with the academics of her time, one could identify each style and the names on the public monuments— most of them lost through general indifference. What for? Nothing was more inimical to Camille Claudel than the borrowed elegance of the members of the Institute. All of them were lackeys, ancient pensioners of the Villa Medici, forever subject to the banal and official statuary of Imperial Rome. They were blind to the Mediterranean light and dumb to the inspiration of the great Italians. What good, then, is it to evoke the half-forgotten names of those draftsmen next to whom Carrier-Belleuse appears like a great innovator and in whose names the very distinguished Carpeaux was condemned for indecency and vulgarity? Camille Claudel, the little village maid, was unfamiliar with this urban art and no more than we do today did she look at it. In Villeneuve, there were none of those "melancholy men in modern dress [who] stain their cheap limestone pedestals with green juice . . . nor naked women . . . hewn out for internment in cemeteries and museums."[†]

[*] E. and J. de Goncourt, *Journal*. (Entry dated May 10, 1894.)
[†] Paul Claudel, "Camille Claudel Statuaire," *Oeuvres en prose* (Paris: Gallimard, 1969), page 273.

To isolate Camille Claudel from her time, to speak of her as a female Rimbaud of sculpture, gleaning from a few contradictory models and instinctively and spontaneously creating an original work, however, would be an error. Camille Claudel was not an autodidact—if that term can be applied to a craft so far removed by its nature from amateurism as is sculpture. For if the biographical material collected to date suggests that Camille Claudel's artistic formation was solitary, unguided and devoid of formal schooling, an even superficial glance at her early works is proof of the contrary: these are perfect works by a dexterous and professional hand. They appear effortless and have none of the heaviness of abandoned drafts.

It is time, then, to pay one's respects to her first master, whom everyone, including Paul Claudel (familiar with the artistic formation of his sister), notes only in passing while, in fact, an examination of styles and the coincidences of place and dates should rank his influence as foremost.

Today, the name of Alfred Boucher evokes few echoes. Nonetheless, he was a talented sculptor who deserves neither to be forgotten nor to have suffered the misfortune of having the Germans, during the Occupation, melt his most famous work, the delicate and at the same time powerful *The Goal* (*Au Bout*)—one of the first modern bronzes to glorify sport.

Alfred Boucher was from Nogent-sur-Seine, or more precisely, from Bouy-sur-Ovin, a few kilometers away. He was the son of a farmhand who became the gardener of the sculptor Ramus. Ramus, who sculpted in the style of the previous century, in the manner of, say, a Clodion, had guessed the talent of his gardener's son and opened his studio to him, and eventually the way to Paris, the Ecole des Beaux-Arts and, finally, the Prix du Salon. This anecdote, however, does not explain the strange coincidence that led Camille Claudel to the famous Paul Dubois—the great-great-nephew of Pigalle and the director of the Ecole des Beaux Arts—who was also from Nogent and who enriched the town with his bronzes. [*]

Ramus knew Dubois, who later helped Boucher at the Ecole des Beaux-Arts and became his friend. There, Boucher joined those artists known as the Florentines, of whom Paul Dubois was the leader. This group of sculptors, like the School of the Great Tuscans, sought to escape romanticism and

[*] There is a Paul Dubois–Alfred Boucher Museum in Nogent.

166

adopted methods similar to those of the Pre-Raphaelites. Although thematically different from the Florentines, Boucher was identified with the movement by his quick and precise style and his taste for a well-made and balanced work.

A creator in his own right, Boucher was a prestigious master as well as a discoverer of talent—perhaps he never forgot his own experience—and in artistic circles, he had a reputation for helping young artists. At the beginning of the century, in an open and communal studio named L'Arche (The Arch), he assembled a number of those artists who would later make up the School of Paris: Chagall, Soutine, Modigliani, Zadkine and Lipchitz. Camille Claudel, however, was one of his earliest discoveries.

The arrival of the Claudel family in Nogent-sur-Seine is crucial because there an artistic vocation that until then had lain dormant became concrete. No doubt Camille's father, an official in the district, saw the two sculptors regularly—certainly Boucher, who remained very attached to the region. They must have seen the same people, gone to the same places—and the modest proof is the bust by Boucher in the museum of Nogent of M. Collin, the Claudel children's tutor. In any event, Camille Claudel, the little peasant girl from Champagne, must have found the ideal master in Boucher. A man of humble origins, he harmoniously combined two opposing tendencies in the sculpture of the period in his own art.

Boucher's works, which can be seen in the museum of Nogent, in the public square, at the cemetery and in the votive chapel (which he bequeathed to his fellow citizens of Bouy-sur-Ovin), are examples of his mastery and his authenticity. *Portrait of His Mother* (*Portrait de sa mère*), a seated peasant woman with gnarled hands, for example, is a masterpiece of nobility and simplicity, as is *Tenderness* (*La Tendresse*), a Donatello-like marble that mingles pity with resignation. The mother is already *Old Helen* and an intimation of *Clotho; Tenderness* foreshadows *The Little Chatelaine*. After Boucher, Camille can be said to be the last of the Florentines and the bearer of an indelible mark that Rodin could never erase. The fact that she was a woman and thus destined to do delicate work brought her that much closer to the finicky art of the first great masters of Florence—the goldsmiths—an art that was very different from the intense and often brutal style that suited Rodin. Younger than Rodin, Camille Claudel, nevertheless,

167

came with a much older tradition to a master obsessed with Michelangelo. In a way, she was older than he in spirit—not the least of the paradoxes that characterized their meeting and their work together.

After Boucher introduced Camille to his friend Rodin, he mysteriously disappeared from her life and so, it would seem, from her memory. She never mentioned him in her correspondence, and in time of trouble she never called on him. Boucher, too, although filled with concern, appears to have lost interest in the fate of his student. Could he have had a more gifted one than Camille, who already at the age of twenty, in 1884, had made that beautiful bust *Young Roman?*[*] Or did Camille offend Boucher or show herself ungrateful now that she knew the rudiments of her craft and once she was introduced to Rodin?

In addition to Boucher's teachings, there were frequent visits to museums in Paris, and for Camille, a little country girl, the Louvre must have been a revelation. The *Torso of a Standing Woman* (*Torse de femme debout*), 1888, is full of antique references, and there was a plaster cast (now lost) very reminiscent of the *métopes d'Olympie.*[†] The secret affinity between Camille Claudel's art and Greek art can be glimpsed in the dreamlike quality of her busts, especially in the one of Rodin, and the composition of her groups into architectural settings. This affinity—Camille's as well as Paul's—to Hellenic art is crucial to understanding the ultimate form of Camille Claudel's art.

Can one also discern the influence of Impressionism in Camille Claudel's work? If one thinks in terms of a Médardo Rosso,[‡] the answer is no. Camille made no attempt to erase form, and there is no trace of luminism—her art is energetic and traditional, and she uses well-defined shapes. Her paintings and drawings, however, do reveal strange obsessions that are essentially impressionistic. No doubt, the heavier materials of sculpture—bronze and marble—distance her from those tendencies. Nevertheless, she is not a complete stranger to the rebirth of artistic creation that became known as Impressionism. Camille shows an instinctive honesty in regard to her models and looks for atmosphere—qualities that place her closer to

[*] *L'Art décoratif*, July 1913, page 32.
[†] Ibid., page 39.
[‡] Médardo Rosso, an Italian sculptor (1859–1928).

168

this new movement and further away from pompous repetitions.* In addition, her humble family origins served to protect her from the snobbish bourgeoisie of the Second Empire and made her more receptive to symbolism. The intellectual circles she later frequented allowed her to maintain these precious attributes and enabled her to escape the mythological and allegorical furbelows of the preceding generation.

In short, the secret of Camille Claudel's art lay in her earth-bound instinct, her love of the land; it was her permanent muse. Camille impressed those who met her with her hoarse voice, her countrified speech, her awkward gestures and her childish ways.[†] She always remained in touch with her roots and never forgot that sculpture is born from "a need to touch, from the almost maternal joy of holding clay in between one's hands."[‡]

And how to explain that this young woman, at the height of her beauty, was attracted to Rodin—that thick, bandy-legged, bearded forty-year-old with an incomparable hand? First, let us point out common ground: the manual work of both of them is very similar if not identical. Each of them sculpts in profile, extracting, like a diamond cutter, the muscular expression of a gesture. There is neither softness nor roundness in the execution. The surfaces of a Camille Claudel, like those of a Rodin, are a tactile pleasure. The glistening bumps and hollows are the natural outcroppings of the fundamental work. The shape is the result of constantly renewed gestures rather than the application of formulas or the collage of worn-out reliefs construed by repetition or rote. The statue emerges not from within but as if wrenched from space, like an ordinary pot or a natural hollow. A Camille Claudel, like a Rodin, has the density of a filled object.

The two styles are also related by their shared defiance with respect to any distortion not inherent in the actual subject. Like Rodin, Camille Claudel attacks from the front; she goes straight to the essence without wasting time on superfluous details, and again, like Rodin, she does not use any

---

* The only recorded aesthetic judgment Camille Claudel made was on the subject of Impressionism: "I don't understand a thing about theoretical questions in matters of art. I just do it. I leave to others—who don't understand it any better than I—the work of discussing these otiose points. Believe me, I'm quite ignorant." E. Claris, *De l'Impressionisme en sculpture* (Paris: La Nouvelle Revue, 1902).
[†] E. and J. de Goncourt, *Journal.* (Entry of March 8, 1894.)
[‡] Henry Asselin, "La Vie douloureuse de Camille Claudel, sculpteur."

props. Her courage in both conception and execution of her work so impressed her contemporaries that they attributed it to a virility unusual in a young woman.

The aesthetics of the two artists, however, are quite different. In Rodin, there is an exacerbation of gesture, a kinetic distortion that prefigures the cinema, a contemporary invention.* Rodin feared immobility. His commentary on Watteau's *Embarkation for Cythera* (*L'Embarquement pour Cythère*) is revealing:

> Have you noticed how this pantomime unfolds? said he to Gsell. Really, is it theater? Is it painting? Hard to say. You can see very well that an artist, when he wants to, can represent not only fleeting gestures but a lengthy action, to use the term current in dramatic art.
>
> It suffices, in order for him to succeed, to dispose of his figures in such a way that the spectator sees those who begin the action, then those who continue it and finally, those who finish it.**

What interested him especially in the painting was the presentation in stages of an integral motion. Likewise, he would have liked to see his *The Burghers of Calais* placed right on the pavement, side by side in a line and like the different stages of the same heroic gesture:

> To intensify this effect, I wanted, you no doubt know it, to fix my statues, one behind the other, in front of the Hôtel de Ville of Calais, right on the cobblestones of the square, like a living chain of suffering and sacrifice. My figures could then have appeared to be moving from the municipal building to the Camp of Edward III; and the people of Calais today would nearly brush elbows with them and be made more conscious of the traditional solidarity that binds them to those heroes. It would, I believe, have made a very strong statement. But they rejected my idea and foisted me with a pedestal, a disgrace as well as a superfluity.†

There was nothing synthetic about Rodin, except for his *Balzac,* and that was exactly what struck Camille Claudel.‡

---

* The first cinematic presentation of the Lumière brothers dates from 1895.
** *Auguste Rodin, L'Art;* commentary compiled by Paul Gsell (Paris: Grasset, 1911), pages 91 ff.
† Ibid., page 115.
‡ Letter from Camille Claudel to Rodin. Archives of Musée Rodin.

One has only to look at *The Gates of Hell* (*La Porte d'enfer*), his life's work, to understand: the sculpture bursts with energy, almost a surfeit of it, which, like a visit to the Rodin Museum, tends to leave one slightly exhausted. In the terms of film language, Rodin practiced incessant "traveling" (dolly shots) while there is nothing like that in Camille Claudel's work, nor for that matter in the works of Rodin's other disciples, who tired of the constant flicker of shapes.

Quite the contrary, Camille Claudel's groups have an air of permanence. The dancers in *The Waltz* don't spin; the spiral that animates them is as immobile as that of a seashell. *Clotho* is a spider caught in its own web. *Çacountala* (*The Abandonment*) is built like a Poussin composition—all the points that seem out of balance compensate one another and refer to a single invisible yet very real point. And although she did indeed tackle some very difficult compositions whose gravitational forces were off center, these works forced her to reestablish the equilibrium of the entire mass. Camille never left them as mere shaky studies; instead she worked them out so that her sculpture took on the intensity of life, sacrificing gesticulation in favor of expression. In Rodin, the opposite phenomenon occurs—he looks for solid equilibrium in the mass. He exchanges movement for theatrical gesture, which he constructs atop an immobile block.

The taut, still power of Camille Claudel's work instantly distinguishes it from comparable works by Rodin. Camille Claudel's sculpture is more traditional, closer to the origins of this art[*]—so that the agnostic, in this sense, is in fact more religious than her master, who, although always invoking God, may be the most profane of sculptors.

Another important difference lies in the very personal manner in which Camille Claudel handles her themes—themes which appear very similar to those of Rodin. The couple and the dance obsessed them both. *The Abandonment* or *Çacountala* has often been compared to *The Eternal Idol* (*L'Eternelle idole*), as has *Clotho*, in a different sense, to *She Who Was the Helmet-Maker's Beautiful Wife* (*Celle qui fut la belle heaulmière*). These comparisons, however, are superficial because the spirits that animate them are

---

[*] Elie Faure criticizes Rodin for never having understood the sculpture of the Middle Ages, nor, for that matter, Greek sculpture. *Histoire de l'art, L'Art moderne*, 2 (Paris: Librairie Générale Française, 1965), page 146.

very dissimilar. For Rodin, the subject often does not really matter (the titles of his works were frequently added later or by a third party).[*] A Rodin sculpture is an instant image; the title is but a signature like the titles of Debussy's *Preludes,* which one can read after the piece has been played. As for his favorite theme, the couple, it is an infinite variation of the same copulation that he purposely never quite shows us. His women, his nymphs, his Danaïds or fauns are always the same "naughty" studio models.

By contrast, Camille Claudel's sculptures are totally devoid of this lubriciousness. Her reserve shows that she can calculate her effects according to her chosen themes because she believes in the significance of the work she creates. The works express a state of divided self, an exchange has occurred, the erotic reveals a tenderness—a far cry from Rodin's caress, which he transforms into a lecherous grab. Although certainly capable of expressing an idea, especially when he had to submit to the discipline of a specific commission—*The Burghers of Calais* and *Balzac* are examples—Rodin mishandled countless subjects because of his inability to conceive and master ideas. *The Thinker* (*Le Penseur*) is a powerful paleontological athlete at rest, but it is easy enough to see that he has a long way to go before he is a Pascal.

So many of Rodin's monuments—*Victor Hugo* and *Claude Lorrain*—fail for the same reason. His best works are the probes into his prolific unconscious, while Camille Claudel's best works are the fruits of her research and careful thought, and they ripen. Each work is the result of a special and renewed attention and is born out of and for the idea it expresses. Process and formula as creative methods are completely foreign to Camille Claudel, as are repetitions and revivals. The figures that comprise her groups are not interchangeable.

Likewise, one is always aware of the perfect equivalence between the size of the work and its subject, which gives an impression of density and balance. Camille Claudel never attempted to create an epic out of a poem. The best example is *The Gossipers,* also known as *The Secret* (*La Confidence*): the little group can be held in one's hand exactly like a secret. This balance

---

[*] But for the intervention of Léon Cladel, *L'Eternelle idole* would have been named "On n'est pas de bois"—"We Are Not Made of Wood."

can be found in yet another form in Camille Claudel's work—the adjustment between sculptor and model in the portraits. It has been said that these works constituted "a major contribution to the art of portraiture in French sculpture because of the mobility of the features at all angles of observation."[*] This is absolutely true. Camille Claudel's busts are conceived in three dimensions (rather than achieving depth by the artificial concave lines of a flat drawing or from the point of view of a flattering angle, the congenital defects of most contemporary busts—which also means that observed from almost any side the angles are dead). Like a face come alive, Camille Claudel's busts multiply their facets as the statue rotates and all the features are incredibly mobile. This "tour de force" much admired in the Italian sculptors of the Quattrocento was like a lost secret, and the traces of a bygone era provide Camille Claudel's busts with a special felicity.

One also has to mention the relationship between Camille Claudel's art and Art Nouveau. No doubt this experiment born from the wish to adopt new processes and materials must have attracted a sculptor whose work was experimental by nature. It is possible that the work of necessity, the confection of lamps and other such utilitarian objects, inspired her in that direction. Art Nouveau, from 1890 and for a few years afterwards, guided Camille Claudel's search for new materials,[†] onyx among others. She made use of the transparency and the network of veins to reinforce lines in the manner of cameo sculptors, and she mingled together materials as well: *Hamadryad* was carved from both marble and bronze and there is an extraordinary version of *The Gossipers* in onyx. The spirit of Art Nouveau also finds expression in the sinuous, semi-vegetal elegance of the drapes which, like ivy, cover the body of the woman in *The Waltz* and the use of a household chimney as an original symbol for meditation in *Deep in Thought*. But the resemblances remain superficial; above all, they show that no artist is a stranger to his time. They do not account for a work whose rigorous observance of measure escapes the excesses of fashion.

In this highly synthesized and carefully calculated art, nothing is accessory. Drapery, for example, plays an essential role in Camille Claudel's work.

[*] Annie Scottez, *Catalogue de l'Exposition La Sculpture Française de 1850–1914 dans les musées et les collections publiques du Nord de la France* (Lille, 1982, page 156).
[†] In a letter to Eugène Blot, Camille Claudel suggests that *La Joueuse de flûte* (*The Flute Player*) sit on an onyx rock. Claudel Fund, Bibliothèque Nationale.

Her statuary, unlike that of Rodin, does not seek nudity *per se*. Almost all the gestures of her figures are accompanied by quick, choppy strokes, receptacles of energy for the group and in contrast to the unconstrained bodies. Like stays on a boat, the drapery provides the balance for the dancers or for *Fortune; Clotho* is stabilized by threads. *The Wave* is itself an autonomous drape which gives the group of bathers authority and significance. In accordance with this systematic method, nudity in the works of Camille Claudel is always deliberate and meaningful: it indicates abandonment (in the sense of letting go) and tenderness—a defenseless state.

The examination of the exterior qualities of Camille Claudel's work, the style and the manner, brings us to the essence of her art—what in fact struck all the critics: its inwardness. Unanimously, all who saw her work were struck by the intensity of her sculpture. It has something withdrawn or folded in on itself, something closed, a melancholy if not an outright sadness, which differentiates it from the work of the sculptors of her generation. In vain, one searches in Camille Claudel's work, to quote Bourdelle's apt expression, for "the central point *where the chariots start*,"[*] and indeed, a Camille Claudel statue is characterized not by a luminosity but by an incandescence. Her works seem to be surrounded by a halo (in this respect, the screen in *The Gossipers,* which meant so much to Camille, is important). This removes us even further from the constrained and pointed atmosphere of Rodin's work. The objective cause of this inwardness must lie in the history of her sculpture; except for the busts, almost all of Camille Claudel's works are interior self-portraits. It is not so surprising then if the works of Camille Claudel often appear melancholy and sad.

Nonetheless, autobiographical data does not explain everything. Alone, it could either slip by unnoticed or outweigh the work. Rather it is the work that counts, her art of modeling clay which transcends whatever one does not know or might have known. Paul Claudel provides a very beautiful definition which expresses better than any other this synthesis, this simultaneous convergence in the work of the great sculptor: "After all, the body knows just as much as the soul, the details of the anatomy are worth those of psychoanalysis, an infinite mass behind that of shapes and movement, passion and ideas, provokes this instantaneous shock."[†]

---

[*] Quoted in I. Jianou, *Bourdelle* (Paris: Arted, 1970), page 47.
[†] Paul Claudel, "Ma soeur Camille" (Preface to the Camille Claudel Exhibition), page 9.

The object modeled is the result of a muscular energy, while that muscular energy, in turn, is the result of a perturbation of the soul; therein lies the ultimate secret of the works of Camille Claudel—works able in an instant to petrify the moment. "Where one would need pages for a score, many scenes for a play, chapters for a novel, to admit us inside that mirror, the miracle of 'simultaneity' illuminates it for us with a single blow to the head."[*]

How better to characterize the work of Camille Claudel than to place it next to that of her contemporaries? Where Bourdelle or Maillol triumphed outside in the light of day, in the streets, in the sunshine of a fresh morning or under sun-speckled clouds, the lamplight of Camille Claudel can easily pass unnoticed. Her domain is not the sun but the shadows inside a house. Just as there is chamber music, so there is chamber sculpture. In his notebooks, Philippe Berthelot perfectly defines the interior art of Camille Claudel:

> Mlle. Claudel's sculpture is very different from Rodin's. She picks and gathers the light like a bouquet, unlike Rodin, who presents a compact block that shoves it back. Now that the sculpture of outdoors and of nudity has no more reason for being, she creates the sculpture of the home which will be the poetic theme, the conscience of the hearth, the center, the living soul of the house: her art (the shades) has an inner light, is perforated, cut out like stained glass, it welcomes and captures the light. It is in this way that her art most resembles the art of jade.[†]

Again and for one last time, we refer to Paul Claudel's commentary on his sister: "Just as a man sitting in the countryside employs, to accompany his meditation, a tree or a rock on which to anchor his eye, so a work by Camille Claudel in the middle of the room is, by its mere form, like those curious stones the Chinese collect: a kind of monument of inner thought, the tuft of a theme accessible to any and every dream. While a book, for example, must be taken from the shelves of the library, or a piece of music must be performed, the worked metal or stone here releases its own incantation, and our chamber is imbued with it."[‡] The poet perceived this quality of "attention" singular to the works of his sister. They are sculptures that one must keep close to one, like poems which one must reread often. Works

[*] Paul Claudel, *Oeuvres en prose*, page 282.
[†] Claudel Fund, Bibliothèque Nationale.
[‡] Paul Claudel, "Camille Claudel statuaire," *L'Art décoratif*, July 1913.

that are deliberately created find their expression equally deliberately and slowly.

It is in this delicate intimacy that is not devoid of intensity and power that the depth and, for some, certainly, the limitation of Camille Claudel's work lie. Some will even see the paradox inherent in the woman sculptor, the kneader, carver of stone and blacksmith all in one, activities far removed from the distaff and the spinning wheel. In addition, those who appreciate symbols may start to dream once they know that Camille, like Vulcan, was handicapped by a slight limp—that the very name Claudel suggests claudication, or lameness. Was the poet likewise aware of it when he made the same handicap a symbol for the fateful steps that led Prouhèze—the ultimate metamorphosis of all women for which Camille Claudel stood as model—to his destiny? Prouhèze, entrusting his satin slipper to the Virgin, cries: "But when I shall try to throw myself in the path of evil, let it be with a lame foot! When I shall want to cross the barrier you have put in my way, let it be with a clipped wing!"[*]

[*] Paul Claudel, *Le Soulier de satin* (*The Satin Slipper*), Scene V, in *Théâtre II* (Paris: Gallimard, 1949), page 685.

176

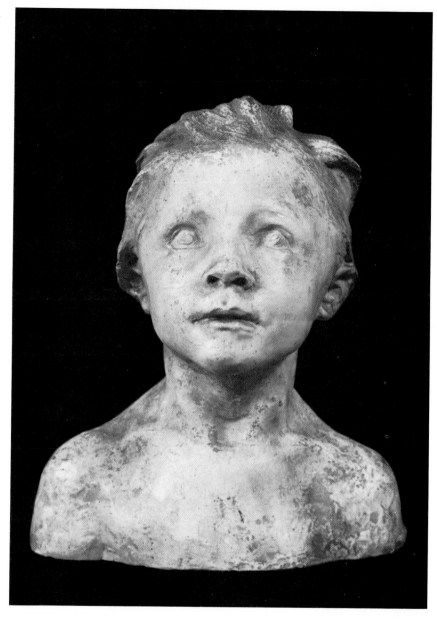

86–88. The Little Chatelaine. *Plaster, 1893,*
13 × 11 × 8½ inches.

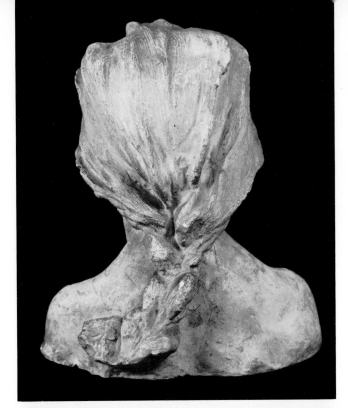

87.

88.

89, 90. The Little Chatelaine. *Marble, 1895,*
13½ × 11¼ × 9 inches.

91.

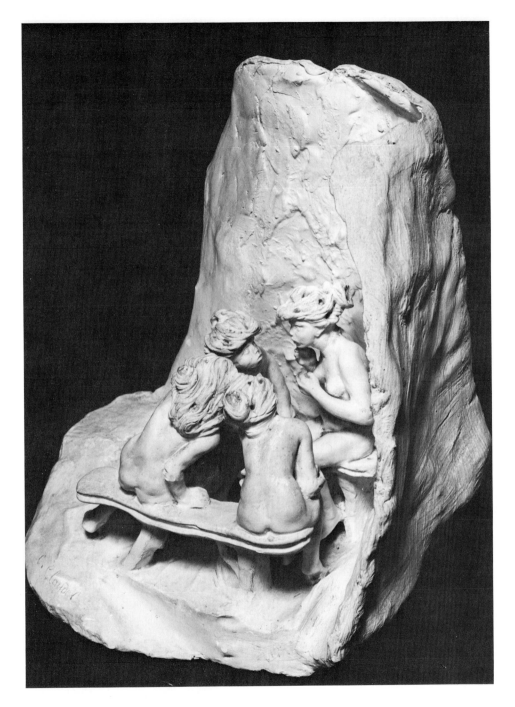

91, 92. The Gossipers. *Plaster, 1894,*
15¾ × 15¾ × 15¾ inches.

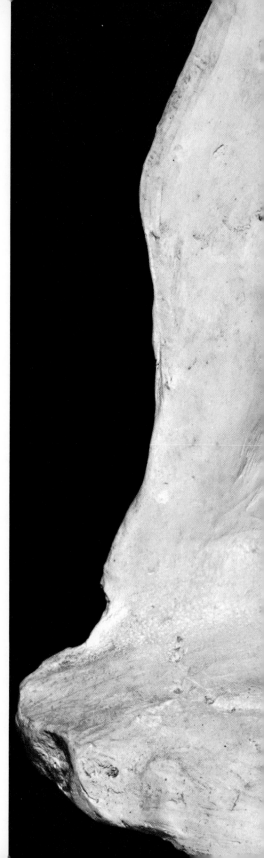

C. Claudel

93. The Gossipers. *Marble and bronze, 1905,*
13 × 13 × 10½ inches.

OPPOSITE: 94. The Gossipers *(detail of marble-and-bronze*
version).

184

95, 96. The Beseecher. *Bronze, 1905,*
24½ × 26 × 14½ inches.

188

97. Maturity. *Plaster, 1895,*
33½ × 65½ × 15¾ inches.

189

98.

99.

*Photos 98–101
show* Maturity
in detail.

102. Maturity. Bronze, 1902, 45 × 64 × 28½ inches.

103.

104.

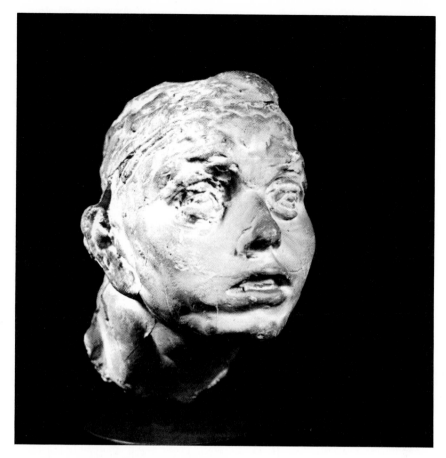

105. Study of a Head. *Plaster, around 1895,*
5¼ × 4 × 5¼ inches.

OPPOSITE, ABOVE: *103. The Vanished God. Plaster, 1894,*
28½ × 15 × 22 inches.

OPPOSITE, BELOW: *104. Sea Foam. Marble and onyx, around 1884*
or between 1892 and 1905; 9¼ × 15¾ × 6 inches.

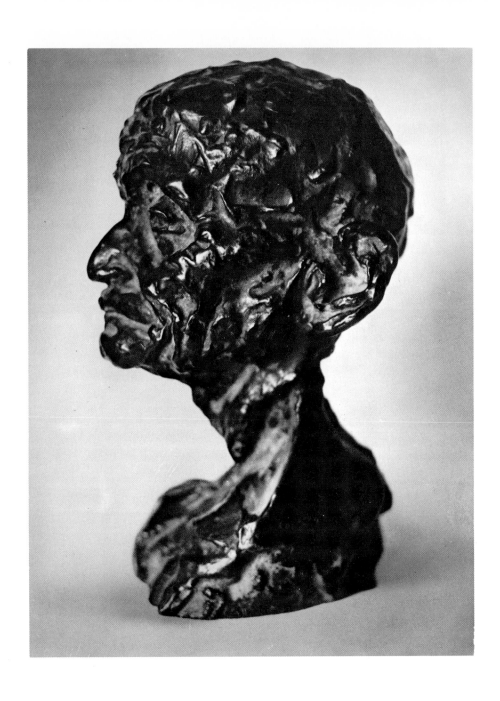

106. Study of a Head for *Maturity. Bronze, around 1895,*
6¾ × 3½ × 4¾ *inches.*

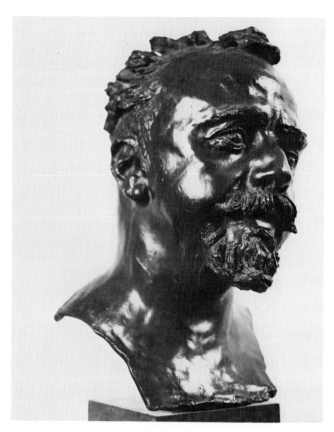

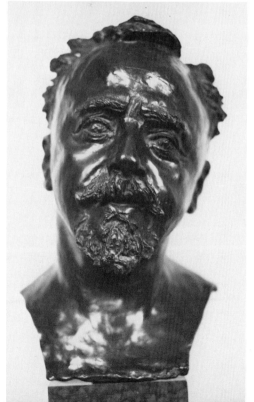

107, 108. Bust of Léon Lhermitte.
Bronze, 1895,
13¾ × 9¾ × 9¾ inches.

109.

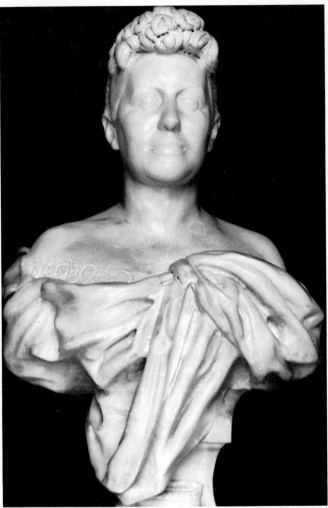

110.

198

109, 110. Countess Arthur de Maigret. *Marble, 1897,*
30¾ × 19 × 14½ inches.

112.

111, 112. Count Christian de Maigret in the Costume of Henry II.
Marble, 1899, 26 × 25½ × 17 inches.

199

113. Perseus and the Gorgon. *Marble, 1902?,*
20½ × 9½ × 9¾ inches.

OPPOSITE: *114*. Perseus and the Gorgon *(detail).*

116.

OPPOSITE: *115.* Perseus and the Gorgon. *Marble, 1902,
77¼ × 43¾ × 39 inches.*

Photos 116–119 show the marble Perseus and the Gorgon
in detail.

203

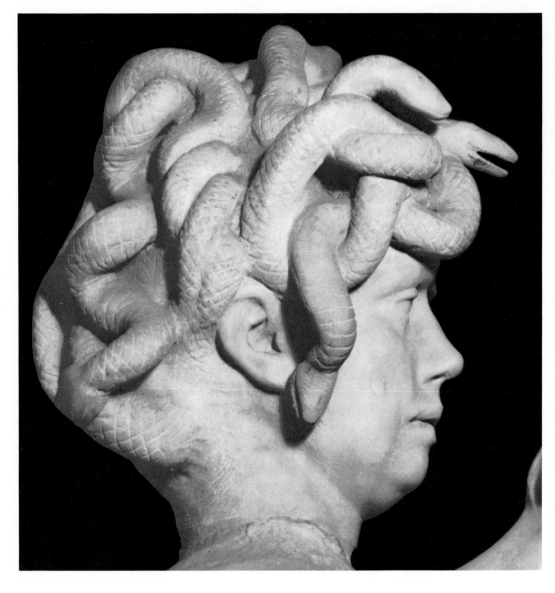

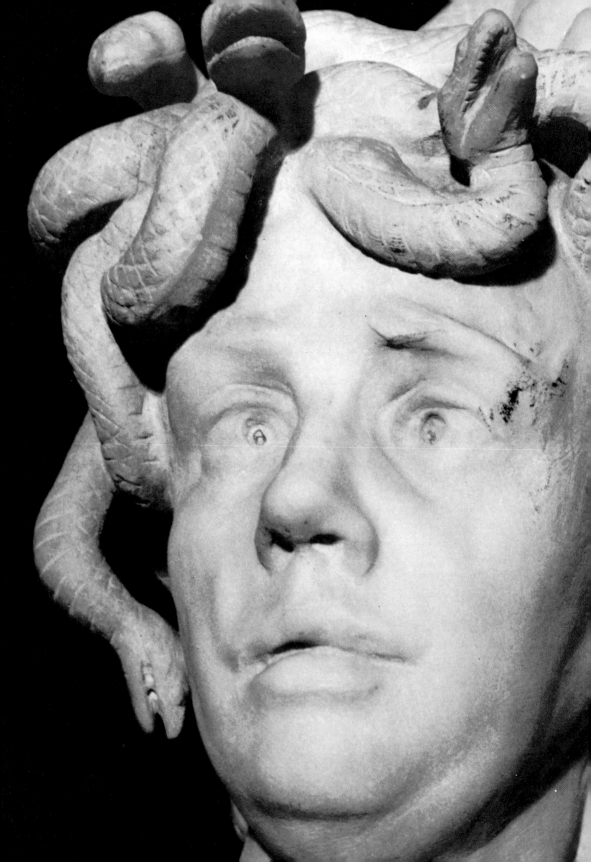

120. Perseus and the Gorgon.
Bronze, 1905,
12¼ × 11¾ × 9¾ inches.

121. Aurora. *Marble, 1905,*
13³⁄₄ × 11¹⁄₂ × 11³⁄₄ inches.

122, 123. Fortune. *Bronze, 1905,*
19 × 11½ × 7 inches.

124. Dream by the Fire. Marble, 1902,
9¼ × 12¼ × 9¾ inches.

125, 126. The Flute Player.
Bronze, before 1905,
21 × 10½ × 9½ inches.

214

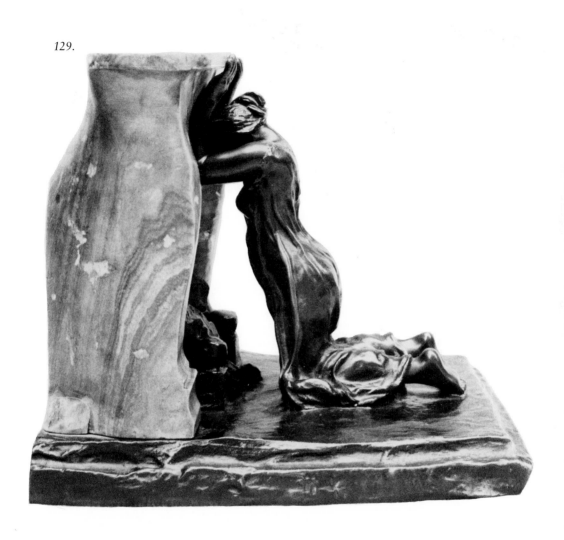

129.

129, 130. Deep in Thought.
*Onyx and bronze with lamp, 1905,
9½ × 8¾ × 10¾ inches.*

Before the Public

"The Pathetic Lot of Sculpture Amongst Painting"

Title of a Daumier caricature

At the end of the nineteenth century, while liberalism prevailed in economic affairs, the art market was carefully controlled. Then, private galleries as we know them today, galleries that promote an artist, guarantee him an annual exhibition and contact with critics, were in their early stages with the exception of a few art dealers such as Durand-Ruel, Vollard, Bing and the exhibitions the Impressionists organized for themselves at Nadar. None of these art dealers, moreover, offered an outlet for sculpture.

The only door left open to sculptors in terms of achieving any kind of recognition was through the salon. Because the salons were patronized by official institutions, they in turn were notorious for their lack of dynamism. The best known and oldest (founded during the Ancien Régime) was the Salon des Artistes Français, which once a year did in fact open its doors at the Palais d'Industrie on the Champs-Elysées. Supported by the officials of the Ecole des Beaux-Arts, the S.A.F. had, over the years, become the repository for banality and immobility. The winners of awards became the members of the jury, received the state commissions, and thus a vicious circle of conventionality was complete.

Like the good polemicist he was, Octave Mirbeau aptly described this system: "A bazaar of mediocrity, a rummage sale of rubbish, a huge fair of miserable failures and impotent self-conceits." Nevertheless, since a considerable number of works were shown there, luck brought together the worst with the better, and sometimes an opportunity was given to original works. And even if these works were barely noticed, admission to the Salon was already of some value. It was a certificate of professionalism and with perseverance, after a couple of years, it might bring the artist an article in the newspaper or a few sales.

Camille Claudel was admitted to the Salon des Artistes Français as early as 1883. Classified as a student of Rodin and Boucher, she exhibited there until 1889. In 1890, she moved to the Société Nationale des Beaux-Arts (S.N.B.A.), which was founded in the same year at the initiative of a few painters and sculptors—among them, Puvis de Chavannes, Meissonier, Carolus Duran and Eugène Carrière—who were disappointed by the S.A.F. The Société Nationale wished to be different in spirit and hoped to escape the sterilizing patronage of the Ecole des Beaux-Arts. The purpose of the salon, which was located on the Champ-de-Mars in the old machinery pavilion of the 1884 Exposition, was to reveal to the public talents that lacked the dubious benefit of the academic training of the Ecole des Beaux-Arts or the approbation of the members of the Institute. Rodin, and for good reason, was one of the most active organizers of this new group. (Sculptors were especially rare since that art was dominated by academism and its free spirits could be counted on the fingers of one hand.)

As a result, most of the sculptors at the S.N.B.A. were the descendants of Rodin and, like all associations, the S.N.B.A. tended to transform itself into a club—a refuge for a new academism. Before that occurred, however, the S.N.B.A. harbored the eccentricities of a new wave of sculptors and attracted wide notice, although it was not frequented by the same critics or the same public.

Until 1903, with only a few rare exceptions, Camille Claudel exhibited at the Société Nationale des Beaux-Arts. Each year the newspapers mentioned her name more or less at length. In 1891, probably thanks to Rodin, Camille became a member of the jury.

The last part of Camille Claudel's career fell under the direction of Eugène

Blot. At the end of the nineteenth century and following in the footsteps of Vollard and Bing, Eugène Blot founded a gallery that quickly became one of the best in Paris. In his showrooms, located on the Boulevard de la Madeleine and rue Richepanse, he exhibited such future celebrities as Bonnard, Marquet, Vuillard and Matisse, next to whom he hung works by Cézanne and Guillaumin as bait. In sculpture, he sponsored—in addition to Camille Claudel—Bernard Hoetger and Carl Milles, a Swedish sculptor influenced by Rodin.

Camille Claudel and Eugène Blot became friends. Eugène Blot was never to forget Camille and remained loyal to her until his death in 1939.

Such is the setting in which Camille Claudel—first with Rodin's help—established her career and acquired the not-so-negligible fame she achieved during her lifetime.

It would be too tedious to reproduce all the excerpts from the press that solidified for her contemporaries Camille's reputation as a sculptor. Out of context and removed from the criticism that her equals and rivals were also subject to, they are of little significance. Likewise, the regularity with which these articles appeared did not necessarily imply that the criticism was always favorable. It was customary then to write a word about all the works exhibited, and since the readership of the time did not yet suffer from a surfeit of printed material, the critics were not afraid of discouraging the public with exhaustive enumerations. In any case, these reviews provided a large stamping ground for future art historians.

From 1888, when she was only twenty-four years old, to 1905, the name of Camille Claudel appears frequently in the press. As long as she remained with Rodin, however, she does not seem to have held the attention of the great critics. Her name is mentioned with indulgence—the kind that second-rate, nearsighted critics with timid judgment reserve for a skillful young artist who does not deserve a classic *cursus honorum*. Although she was already showing them perfect works, masterpieces such as *Çacountala*, they complained about "an uneven execution," but it was easy enough to recognize the powerful and amazing inspiration of such a young woman.

After 1893 the most famous critics of the time began to notice Camille and extol her name. By the turn of the century, Roger Marx, Octave Mirbeau, Henri de Braisne, Gustave Geffroy, Gustave Kahn and Camille

Mauclair—to mention only the names of those whose reputations are not completely lost to us today—were all celebrating the name of Camille Claudel. But one also has to take into account the hyperbole of the times or the cult of art and its high priests, the geniuses—or at least those who were considered such without much effort on their part—who took their cue from the intellectuals and were determined to redress a religion in demise, indeed in disgrace. Nonetheless, the fact remains that for nearly ten years each of Camille's showings at the salon was showered with praise. Together, all these articles form a portrait, or better yet, a caricature, and it is interesting to compare them with the praise Camille Claudel received from the two authentic apostles of her art—Mathias Morhardt and Paul Claudel.

"Caricature" seems appropriate because all the critics saw only the sex of the sculptor. That a woman could sculpt like a man and in such a nonanecdotal fashion astounded them. Where we see balance and measure, they perceived torsion, fever and romantic passion—in the manner of Rodin and with his exaggerated style. They attributed the "savagery" of certain of her groups to her "rustic origins," while others found in them a "poignant sadness." It is true that the unusual vitality and nervous energy of Camille's works sliced through the dull compositions of the decadents just as the interior tensions distinguished them from the insubstantial flights and aesthete draperies of Art Nouveau. But it was by virtue of the dwindling standards of criticism rather than her style that she was compared to Constantin Meunier, Escoula and Bourdelle. The more perspicacious among the critics observed traces of archaism, signs of tradition—in other words, the French sculpture of the past—and in particular Ligier Richier (1500–1567) was mentioned several times. The severest critics reproached her for excessive modeling, a lack of gentleness in her evocation of femininity or yet again of being a "loner," and we can detect the signs of slight anxiety that originality always produces. With time, however, these judgments become flattering.

By the beginning of the century, several critics, and not the worst among them, no longer hesitated to use the word "genius," which Octave Mirbeau had already uttered in 1895. In 1901, Camille Mauclair, the high priest of critics, spoke of "a ray of geniality . . . a mental atmosphere which resembles it. Camille Claudel," he concluded, "is the most considerable woman artist at the present hour." Gustave Kahn, perhaps the king of critics, in 1905 solemnly placed her next to Berthe Morisot as "the authentic representative of the female genius." But that was already the year of Camille's dusk. Just as she was approaching fame and even fortune, she was treading the path toward darkness, bearing her cross, and none of these odes was of any use to her.

Let us bring this brief chapter to a close with a homage to Mathias Morhardt, and to Paul Claudel, art critic.

The article that Mathias Morhardt published in March 1898 is the first work dedicated completely to Camille Claudel. It was the only one for more than eighty years (nearly a century!). These fifty or so pages of small print and close type are the Old Testament for all studies of Camille Claudel. These pages, which we know were written in the company of the artist herself, offer us a kind of confidential portrait, a disguised interview of sorts. They reveal all the ideas that have since been suggested or developed on the relationship between Rodin and Camille, on the influence of Greek and Asian art, on the newness of this intimate art form. Both friendship and intelligence inspired this text, which remains without equal.

Just as significant in a whole other sense are the articles that Paul Claudel wrote about his sister. These are collected in *L'Oeil écoute*. Rather than art criticism, they are meditations by an amateur and an intimate observer. Everything that Mathias never said about the interior virtues of her work is therein revealed. Although reference texts today, Claudel's articles were without much significance when they first appeared. In 1905, the date when his first essay on his sister's work was published in *L'Occident*, the poet was as yet barely known. In 1951, the date of the first Camille Claudel exhibition, organized at the Musée Rodin, Camille's fame was obscured by her brother's, and his homage to his sister was perceived as just another family affair and of little interest. Today, when the work of Camille Claudel is at last being recognized, Paul Claudel's texts merit rereading as essential testimony.

Chapter 9

Camille Claudel Today

We have already mentioned that Rodin hoped that a room in the Hôtel Biron—the museum the Republic of France established in his honor—could be devoted to Camille Claudel and that it would bear her name. The idea came from Mathias Morhardt and Rodin agreed to it immediately. Her principal sculptures would be brought together under his paternal protection—the way he might assemble the works of an adopted child. In the end, mishap and administrative paralysis caused the project to be aborted.

If no site exists today where one can get a panoramic view of Camille Claudel's work, at least its dispersion allows her to escape physically from Rodin's clutches. Nevertheless, one wonders whether her work has really attained a spiritual autonomy.

Do Camille Claudel's manner, style and search really provide us with a unique truth that is viable today after so many upheavals, so many often gratuitous and insignificant innovations have transformed our taste? Or is Camille Claudel destined only to attract the habitués of auction houses, the experts and the collectors certain of discovering in her scattered work a rare merchandise whose price is bound to rise?

Or does the vital energy of her work survive intact? After nearly a century, does the subtle and fragile flame of the eternally young woman still burn and kindle the interest of the viewer today? Can one find repose beside that gentle light after having traveled through shapeless landscapes, beside that pure form after architectural distortions have exploded one's notion of sculpture?

As we near the end of this study, we must try to answer some of these questions.

When Camille put down her tools, sculptors were already changing their ways. This Janus period built on the ruins of academism was dividing them—some adopted a neoclassicism devoid of all romanticism, while others resolutely turned their backs on the past. Rodin died a second time. Today, his sculpture is viewed like the work of an ancient tutelary; even his flaws are considered monuments. To reduce Camille Claudel to the dimensions of an exquisite chapel inside a Rodin cathedral would be one way of immortalizing her—but a mistake, surely. Instead, we hope that our effort will contribute to restoring Camille Claudel's autonomy at the risk, perhaps, of exposing her to the condescension of art historians.

Because her illness kept her from venturing very far, her work may, in fact, appear timid and from another era. Some people will reproach her for not having known how to break off totally from Rodin—with her reason rather than with just her emotion—others, of looking for her sources of inspiration in the present rather than in the future that was unfolding before her eyes. Others, bolder yet, will reproach her for not knowing how to incorporate her madness into her work, thus leaving us disquieting revelations, like old Goya—of managing, in other words, to keep her steady hand despite her troubled spirit.

All these accusations are quite false: the work of Camille Claudel acquires its energy and uniqueness from an instinctive resurgence to tradition rather than from its association with the tendencies of the time. To compare her with the innovators of her generation would be a disservice; neither would it explain their merits.

The work of Camille Claudel is an island, a conservatory for rare species. Although her themes may be limited, they are never anecdotal and therefore achieve their fullness of expression. They are passionately developed obsessions, the record of the adventures of the female soul: her family, love and childhood.

Her style is defined by her remarkable manual dexterity and again, although not quite original—the outside influences are obvious—the work nevertheless attains its uniqueness by her sincere and spontaneous touch. Camille Claudel is a paradox, and her work is the confession of a proud consciousness that achieves equilibrium where inward experience meets the universal.

She is one of the last of the great humanist sculptors. Shaped by classical culture, her life was determined by a personal tragedy and a world committed to destroying her. But there is nothing heroic about her art: no stela raised to the dead, no pure architecture, no hymn to the body; nor is she kin to Bourdelle, Despiau or Maillol, the most illustrious Frenchmen of her day. She neither announces nor paves a new way.

Instead, Camille Claudel's art is a manifestation of man's romantic dream. Her work stands alone and will appeal only to those for whom art is still the representation of human emotions. For them, the lively freshness of her busts, the natural and almost earthy sensuality of her bodies and faces that contrasts with the quasi-Asiatic elegance of the surfaces and the gesticulation of the figures—therein is expressed the bittersweetness of life, as savored by a woman.

Catalog of Works

The relative obscurity in which the work of Camille Claudel remained for such a long time inevitably leads to difficulties and lacunae in establishing a definitive catalog. The works that have not been located are verified by bibliographical references. We believe that several essential works (notably *Hamadryad* and a marble *Clotho*) were not destroyed and will be uncovered one day soon, thanks to the resurgent interest of contemporary art collectors and enthusiasts to which, it is hoped, this book will contribute.

1876– 1877	*Bismarck, Napoleon I, David and Goliath* (*Bismarck, Napoléon 1er, David et Goliath*) Clay study. Found recently. Attributed to Camille Claudel.
Around 1880	*Diana* (*Diane*) Plaster. Private collection.
1881	*Young Roman* (*Paul Claudel at Thirteen Years of Age*) (*Jeune romain*) Plaster. Disappeared. Bronze. Red marble pedestal signed in the back *C. Claudel*. It was cast for the Baroness Nathaniel de Rothschild. In 1903 it was given to the Musée Bertrand de Chateauroux (a gift of Baron Alphonse de Rothschild).

1882   *Old Helen (Bust of an Old Woman)* (*La Vieille Hélène*)
        Plaster. Private collection.
        Terra cotta. Exhibited at the Salon des Artistes Français in 1885
        under the title *Old Woman*.
        Bronze. Cast by Fumière and Gavignot. Private collection. According
        to M. Morhardt, there were several versions in terra cotta and in
        plaster with modifications in the hairdo. Almost all these versions
        are now in the United States. There are also several verified bronzes.

1883   *Bust of a Woman (Portrait of Mme. B.)* (*Buste de femme*)
        Plaster. Signed *Camille C.* on the left shoulder. Disappeared.

1884   *Torso of a Crouching Woman* (*Torse de femme accroupie*)
        Tinted plaster. Shown at the Camille Claudel Exhibition, Musée
        Rodin, in 1951.
        Bronzes. Private collections. Unsigned. Founder's name lacking.

        Torso of an Old Woman Standing. (*Torse de vieille femme debout*)
        Plaster. Private collections.

        Bust of Louis-Prosper Claudel (*Buste de Louis-Prosper Claudel*)
        Plaster? Disappeared.

        Young Roman (My Brother at Sixteen) (*Jeune romain*)
        Plasters. According to M. Morhardt, there were several copies, one
        of which belonged to Marcel Schwob.
        Bronzes. Signed *Camille Claudel* at the bottom of the left shoulder.
        A first casting was given by the Baron Alphonse de Rothschild to
        the Musée d'Art et d'Archéologie in Toulon in 1899. A second
        casting done for the Baroness Nathaniel de Rothschild, his sister,
        was given by him to the Musée Calvet in Avignon in 1897. A
        third copy was given by the same donor to the Musée de Tourcoing,
        exhibited in 1978, and then sent to the Musée des Beaux-Arts et
        de la Dentelle in Calais.

        Portrait of Louise-Athanaïse Claudel (*Portrait de Louise-Athanaïse
        Claudel*)
        Oil. Destroyed.

Around *Bust of a Woman with Closed Eyes* (*Buste de femme aux yeux
1884   clos*)
        Terra cotta. Unsigned. Given by the Claudel family to the Abbot
        Alphonse Godet when he was the parish priest in Villeneuve-sur-
        Fère, between 1914 and 1919. Private collection.

226

Sea Foam (L'Écume)
Marble and onyx. Signed *Camille Claudel*. The dating of this work
is highly problematical. Because of its subject matter, one is tempted
to situate it in the tradition of Alfred Boucher or within the teaching
of the Colarossi Academy; but, by the combination of materials
it incorporates, it could belong to the years of solitude (1892–
1905) when Camille was seeking her way in a slightly precious
Art Nouveau style. Private collection.

1885   *Bust of Louise Claudel* (*Bust of a Young Girl*) (*Buste de Louise
Claudel*)
Terra cotta. Gift of Léon Gauchez to the Musée des Beaux-Arts,
Lille, in 1892.
Plaster. Belonged to Samuel Bing. Disappeared.
Bronze, 1886. Unsigned. Gift of the Baroness Nathaniel de Rothschild
to the Musée Bargoin, Clermont-Ferrand, in 1886 or 1887.

Giganti (*Laborer. Head of a Bandit*)
Plaster.
Bronzes. Signed *Camille Claudel*. Musée des Beaux-Arts, Lille (gift
of Alphonse de Rothschild, 1892); Musée de Cherbourg; and private
collection.

Jessie Lipscomb
Terra cotta. Private collection.

Around   *Study of a Hand* (*Étude de main*)
1885   Plaster. Disappeared.
Bronze. Signed *C. Claudel*. Private collection.

Study of a Head (*Étude de tête*)
Plaster. Private collection. Rediscovered in Villeneuve, this study is
the counterpart of Avarice in Rodin's group *Avarice and Lewdness*
(around 1885), which figures in *The Gates of Hell*.

Study of a Head (*Étude de tête*)
Plaster. Private collection. This little head seems to be an echo of
the great *Saint John the Baptist* by Rodin.

Man with His Arms Crossed (*L'Homme aux bras croisés*)
Terra cotta. Study. Private collection.

1886–   *Drawings*
1888   Charcoal. Two series executed at Gérardmer and at the Isle of Wight

published in *L'Art,* vol. 13, no. 2 (1886, 1887 and 1888). One of the originals, *Mennie de Gérardmer,* dated August 29, 1885, can be found at the Musée Boudin, Honfleur, and was given in 1891 by Baron Alphonse de Rothschild.

1886   *Young Roman (Paul Claudel at Eighteen Years of Age) (Jeune romain)*
Plaster. The original was tinted by the artist. Private collection.

Portrait of Jessie Lipscomb (Portrait de Jessie Lipscomb)
Charcoal.

Man Leaning (L'Homme penché)
Plaster. Study. Private collection.
Bronze. 1987. Delval foundry.

1887   *Eugénie Plé*
Oil. Reproduced in *L'Art décoratif,* July 1913. Disappeared.

Portrait of Maria Paillette (Portrait de Maria Paillette)
Oil. Private collection.

Portrait of Rodin Reading a Book (Portrait de Rodin lisant un livre)
Oil. Belonged to Louis-Prosper Claudel. Cited by M. Morhardt. Disappeared.

Around   *Louise Claudel (Madame de Massary)*
1887   Pastel. Private collection.

Portrait of Rodin (Portrait de Rodin)
Charcoal. Private collection.

Portrait of Victoire Joséphine Brunet (Portrait de Victoire Joséphine Brunet)
Oil. Cited by M. Morhardt. Disappeared.

1888   *Bust of Rodin (Buste de Rodin)*
Terra cotta. Disappeared. See the correspondence between Mme. Armand Bloch and the curator of the Musée Rodin in 1932 (Archives of the Musée Rodin).
Plasters. Musée Rodin and Musée Ziem in Martigues.
Bronzes. A copy belonging to Rodin was exhibited at the Société Nationale des Beaux-Arts in 1892, following which the *Mercure de France* produced fifteen more copies, cast by Rudier and num-

bered from one to fifteen. They are marked by a caduceus and signed *Camille Claudel*. Another copy was sold by the artist to Karl Boës, who owned a gallery on the rue des Ecoles according to a piece of correspondence preserved at the Bibliothèque Littéraire Jacques Doucet. In addition, copies are at the Musée de Guéret, legacy of Dr. Benjamin Bord, 1954; Musée Rodin, gift of Rudier, 1950; Musée du Petit Palais, gift of Seligman, 1924; Musée d'Aurillac, as of 1968 after the legacy of d'H. Mondor.

Profile of Auguste Rodin (Profil d'Auguste Rodin)
Bas-relief. Signed *C. Claudel*. Ogiwara Museum, Japan.

Çacountala (The Abandonment. Vertumnus and Pomona)
Tinted plaster. Original signed *Camille Claudel* on the base. Gift of the artist to the Musée de Chateauroux in 1895. One bronze was cast from this by the Delval foundry in 1987.
Terra cotta. Two trial versions exist. Private collections.
Bronzes. 1905. Casting done by Eugène Blot in two sizes from plaster molds which have since disappeared; twenty-five were made from the larger mold, fifty from the smaller one. No. 8 of the larger cast was bought by the French government in 1907 and allocated to the Musée de Cambrai in 1932. The casting belonging to the Musée de Poitiers was a donation from Brisson-Happe; it is from the second series, acquired during the Eugène Blot sale, April 23, 1937. Copies in private collections.
Marble. 1905. Executed for the Countess de Maigret and exhibited in 1905 at the Salon des Artistes Français under the title *Vertumnus and Pomona (Vertumne et Pomone)*. Afterwards, it was bought by Philippe Berthelot and willed to Paul Claudel, who gave it to the Musée Rodin in 1952.

Study after Nature (Étude d'après nature)
Charcoal. Reproduced in *L'Art*, vol. 13, no. 2 (1888).

Ferdinand de Massary
Plaster. Private collection.
Bronzes. Two castings remain. Private collections.

Paul Claudel
Colored pencil. Private collection.

Torso of a Standing Woman (Torse de femme debout)
Plaster. Reproduced in *L'Art décoratif*, July 1913. It belonged to Mr. Henry Lerolle at the time.
Bronze. Signed *C. Claudel*; casting by P. Converset. Private collection.

1889   *Charles Lhermitte as a Child (Charles Lhermitte enfant)*
Plaster.
Bronze. Signed *C. Claudel. Gruet Founder* on the left shoulder. Private collection.

Psalm (Young Girl with a Hood. The Prayer) (Psaulme)
Plaster. Disappeared.
Bronze. Signed *C. Claudel* on the left-hand side of the pedestal. Bought by the Baroness Nathaniel de Rothschild and given to the Musée de Lille; later transferred to the Musée Boucher de Perthes d'Abbeville, where it is today.

Around 1890   *Cat Stretching (Chat s'étirant)*
Bronze. Green patina. Private collection.

Young Woman with a Sheaf (Jeune fille à la gerbe)
Terra cotta. Signed *C. Claudel* on the pedestal. Private collection.
Bronzes. Signed *C. Claudel.* Cast by the Fonderies d'Art Coubertin, 1983. Private collection.

Around 1892   *Study for a Head (Étude de tête)*
Plaster. Private collection.

1892   *The Waltz (La Valse)*
FIRST VERSION:
Plaster. Original disappeared. Signed *Camille Claudel* on the base. It was exhibited in Paris in 1893, at which time it was the property of M. Siot-Decauville, art publisher.
Marble. Foreseen as a government commission (Archives Nationales), it was never accepted.
Bronze. Reduced, it was produced thanks to the efforts of M. Siot-Decauville and later sold to Eugène Blot.
SECOND VERSION:
Plasters. Cited by M. Morhardt, who also mentions twelve castings, variants of this version, and bought by Louis Julien, Georges Hugo, Georges Lorrain and Robert Godet. Only one exists today, the property of Mme. Alexandra Qvale, the granddaughter of the Norwegian painter Fritz Thaulow; it was a gift from Rodin to his painter friend.
Bronzes. Several casts were made, thanks to Mme. Menard and one M.X., according to M. Morhardt; they date from before 1898. Two castings, without the mark of the foundry, are at the Musée Ste. Croix, Poitiers (donation of Brisson, 1953), and at the Musée

Rodin (1963 acquisition). In 1905, Eugène Blot reportedly had fifty castings made for the Camille Claudel/Bernard Hoetger exhibition in his gallery (number given in his catalog; it appears that fewer than this were actually made). No. 5, signed *C. Claudel* on the base on the left, is now in a private collection. Other castings, one from the Alexis Rudier foundry, are in private collections. A bronze enlargement (about thirty-six inches in height) bearing the mark of the founder A. Valsuani exists.

Gilded bronze. The catalog to the Eugène Blot exhibition in 1908 indicates a series in gilded bronze limited to twenty-five, but this was never made.

Oxidized stoneware. A casting was executed by Emile Muller. It was exhibited in 1896 in Paris at the Salon de l'Art Nouveau at Samuel Bing's. Disappeared.

1893   *Clotho (The Fate)*
Plaster. Musée Rodin.
Marble. 1897. Commissioned from Camille Claudel after the banquet in honor of Puvis de Chavannes, January 16, 1895, and intended for the Musée de Luxembourg. Puvis de Chavannes, Auguste Rodin and Albert Besnard were among the subscribers. Mathias Morhardt, Judith Cladel and others made inquiries to the government about the fate of the work, but these proved useless. An important dossier on this subject is in the Claudel Bequest at the Bibliothèque Nationale.
Bronze. Private collection.

The Little Chatelaine (Jeanne as a Child. The Inspired One) (La Petite châtelaine)
Plasters. The original can be found in a private collection. Several others can be found in private collections, including one in tinted plaster that belongs to Mme. Qvale, Thaulow's granddaughter.
Bronzes. 1894. Several casts were made. One casting was given by Alphonse de Rothschild to the Musée Joseph Denais, Beaufort-en-Vallée; another is in a private collection.
Marbles.
1895. A version (the property of Mme. Escudier) and a replica (property of Johany Peytel, acquired in 1968 by the Musée Rodin) were reproduced in *L'Art décoratif,* July 1910.
1896. Of this version, which differs from the first in the treatment of the hair, there is a single example, reproduced in *L'Art décoratif,* July 1913, which belonged then to M. Henri Fontaine. It disappeared for a long time, then was acquired in the early 1980's by

an amateur at a sale where it was presented as a marble without much interest by "a certain Claudel" and bought for 100 francs. Private collection.

1987. Valsuani, founder. Private collections.

1894   *The Gossipers (The Secret) (Les Causeuses)*

Plasters. The original was exhibited at the Musée Rodin in 1951; it belonged to Philippe Berthelot. Private collection. There is a version with a screen in the Musée d'Art et d'Histoire, Geneva. From the original marble several others were made in plaster molded with gelatin.

Marbles. According to M. Morhardt, one was executed in 1896 for the Norwegian painter Fritz Thaulow, and another was made without a screen for the architect Pontrémoli. He also states that several statues were acquired by the Musée de Genève, Rodin, Octave Mirbeau, Gustave Geffroy and Robert Godet.

Onyx and bronze. 1897. A single example is known. Belonged once to M. André Peytel. Acquired by the Musée Rodin in 1963.

Bronzes. Eugène Blot reportedly had fifty cast in bronze from the first plaster mold, according to the catalog of the Camille Claudel/Bernard Hoetger exhibit in 1905, but it is possible that not all were made. No. 1 was sold at Sotheby's, London, on June 29, 1983. There is another one with no screen at the Musée Rodin, cast by Georges Rudier. A number of bronzes were cast in 1987 by A. Valsuani.

Marble and bronze. For his personal collection, Eugène Blot had one cast in bronze with a marble screen. Private collection.

Starving Dog (Dog gnawing on a Bone) (Chien affamé)

Plaster. Around 1894. Signed on the pedestal. Private collection.

Bronzes. Two can be found in private collections; one of them has a green patina and bears the mark of the founder, Alexis Rudier, and the signature of Camille Claudel on the pedestal.

The Beseecher (L'Implorante)

Medium unknown. This figure is part of *Maturity*.

Plaster. It belonged to Mlle. Alix Vaissier and is mentioned in the catalog to the Camille Claudel Exhibit at the Musée Rodin in 1951. It has not been found.

Bronzes. Under the title *Beseeching,* twenty were cast in the size of the original and one hundred in reduced size for the 1905 exhibit at the Eugène Blot Gallery. Several are in private collections. The Musée Rodin and the Musée de Bagnols-sur-Cèze (gift of Georges and Adèle Besson) each owns one of the smaller sculptures.

The Vanished God (Le Dieu envolé)
Plaster. Heretofore confused with *The Beseecher.*
Bronze. 1987, by the founder A. Valsuani.

The Painter (Le Peintre)
Plaster. Several examples in private collections.
Bronze. Cited by M. Morhardt as being exhibited in 1897.

Around 1894
First Steps (Premiers pas)
Medium unknown. Work cited in the *Catalogue de l'Exposition de la Libre Esthétique*, Brussels, 1894. Disappeared.

Before 1895
Study of a Head for Old Age (Head of an Old Man) (Étude de tête pour l'Age mûr)
Bronze. Signed *C. Claudel* on the left shoulder; includes the mark of the founder Alexis Rudier. Private collection.

1895
Maturity (Life's Way) (L'Age mûr)

FIRST VERSION:
Plaster. 1895. Commissioned by the government, this work was rejected. Paul Claudel gave it to the Musée Rodin in 1952.

SECOND VERSION:
Plaster. 1898. The second version was accepted by the government, but Camille Claudel never delivered it.
Bronzes. In June 1899, the text for the government commission of a casting in bronze was prepared, then canceled. The first casting was made thanks to Captain Louis Tissier and was executed by the Maison Thiébaut Frères. It was finished in 1902. It bears the inscription *C. Claudel* on the front in the middle of the base, and *Thiébaut frères. Fumière et Gavière. S. Paris.* on the crest of the wave. Owned by the Musée d'Orsay (acquired in 1982). Eugène Blot made a second cast of six and exhibited them in his gallery in 1907. The last person to commission the work was Philippe Berthelot; the founding was executed by Carvilhani, using the plaster model that had remained in the artist's studio. Musée Rodin (gift of Paul Claudel, 1952).

Bust of Léon Lhermitte (Buste de Léon Lhermitte)
Bronze. Private collection.

Bust of Monsieur Pontrémoli (Buste de Monsieur Pontrémoli)
Bronze. See M. Morhardt's letter to Rodin (Archives Musée Rodin). Disappeared.

Study of a Japanese (Étude d'après un japonais)
Plaster. Reproduced in *L'Art décoratif,* July 1913. Disappeared.

Around
1895

Study of a Head (Étude de tête)
Plaster. Private collection.

Woman at Her Dressing Table (Femme à sa toilette)
Plaster. Sketch. Private collection.

Between
1895
and
1898

Blind Singer (Aveugle chantant)
Plaster. Private collection.

Old Blind Singer (Vieil aveugle chantant)
Bronze. Reproduced in *L'Art décoratif,* July 1913.

1897

Countess Arthur de Maigret (La Comtesse Arthur de Maigret)
Plaster. Signed *Camille C.* on the left shoulder.
Marble. Signed *C. Claudel* on the pedestal on the left. Private collection.

Study of a Head (Étude de tête)
Plaster. Private collection.
Bronze. It belonged to Henry Lerolle.

Hamadryad (Young Girl with Water Lilies. Ophelia) (Hamadryade)
Marble and bronze. Produced by Maurice Fenaille, well-known collector and patron of the arts who bought several of Camille Claudel's works.

The Wave (Bathers) (La Vague)
Plaster. Exhibited at the S.N.B.A. in 1897. It seems to have belonged to M. Morhardt and been sold by him to Rodin (Archives of the Musée Rodin).
Bronze and onyx. 1898. Unique, this sculpture was commissioned by Maurice Fenaille, the collector and arts patron. Private collection.

Around
1897

Louis-Prosper Claudel
Pencil. Private collection.

Before
1898

Daphnis and Chloe (Daphnis et Chloé)
Plaster(?). Work cited by M. Morhardt. Seen at the artist's studio. Disappeared.

1898

Perseus and the Gorgon (Persée et la Gorgone)
Plasters. Top half reproduced in *L'Art décoratif,* July 1913. Life-size. Exhibited in 1899.

234

Marbles. Life-size. Exhibited in 1902. Private collection. A smaller version was acquired by the Musée Rodin in 1963.
Bronzes. 1905. Eugène Blot had twenty-five cast. Signed C. *Claudel* on the pedestal. Private collection.

Deep in Thought (Woman Kneeling Before a Hearth) (La Profonde pensée)
Bronze. Exhibited in 1898, then the property of M. André Peytel. Disappeared. Private collection.
Marble. 1900. Reproduced in *L'Art décoratif,* July 1913.
Bronze and onyx. 1905. Cast by Eugène Blot. Signed C. *Claudel* on the base. Shown at the Eugène Blot Gallery in 1905.

Death of a Little Girl with Doves (Little Girl with Doves) (La Jeune fille morte aux colombes)
Oil. Private collection.

1899   *Count Christian de Maigret in the Costume of Henry II (Le Comte Christian de Maigret en costume Henri II)*
Marble. Signed C. *Claudel* on the pedestal at the back. Private collection.

Drawings
Drypoint etching. Two illustrations for Léon Millard's book *Auguste Rodin, Statuary* (Paris: H. Feury, 1899).

Around   *Bust of a Woman (Buste de femme)*
1899   Plaster with a patina. Signed C. *Claudel* on left shoulder. Private collection.

1900   *Fortune (La Fortune)*
Plaster. Disappeared.
Bronzes. According to the catalog to the Camille Claudel show at the Eugène Blot Gallery in 1905, fifty were cast. According to the catalog for the Exhibition of 1908, only twenty-five were made. No. 9 is at the Musée Ste. Croix in Poitiers, a gift of André Brisson, and is signed C. *Claudel* on the wheel. No. 2 is in a private collection and is signed C. *Claudel* on the right side of the base.

Dream by the Fire (Woman Seated Before a Hearth. Intimacy) (Rêve au coin du feu).
Plaster. Exhibited at the Universal Exposition of 1900.
Marble. 1902. Bought by Alphonse de Rothschild and given to the Musée de Draguignan in 1903. Private collection.

Bronzes. Twenty-five were announced by Eugène Blot but never realized.

Woman on the Sofa (Femme au divan)
Oil on canvas. Recently discovered. Private collection.

After 1900
Yule Log (Bûche de Noël)
This work could be *Deep in Thought* or the *Woman Kneeling Before a Hearth*.
Marble. Cited in Camille Claudel's letter to Karl Boës, publisher of the newspaper *La Plume*.

1902
The Alsatian Woman (L'Alsacienne)
Terra cotta with a silver patina. Three-quarters life-size. Exhibited in 1902. Could be *La Vieille Hélène*, since the model was Alsatian.

Portrait of the Countess de Maigret (Portrait de la Comtesse de Maigret)
Drawing. Musée de Château-Gontier.

Before 1905
The Flute Player (The Little Siren. The Siren) (La Joueuse de flûte)
Plaster.
Bronzes. Casting limited to thirty, according to the catalog of the Camille Claudel/Bernard Hoetger Exhibition, but in fact the casting was never done. Private collections.

1905
Aurora (L'Aurore)
Marbles. There are two: one was bought by Eugène Blot at the sale by Fritz Thaulow in 1907; the other is in a private collection.
Bronzes. Twenty-five were cast according to the catalog of the 1908 show at the Eugène Blot Gallery, but the casting was never done.

Bust of Paul Claudel at Thirty-seven Years (Buste de Paul Claudel à trente-sept ans)
Plaster. Private collection.

Study of a Head (Étude de tête)
Plaster. Reproduced in *L'Art décoratif*, July 1913.
Bronze. Signed *C. Claudel* in back. Mark of the founder Eugène Blot. Private collection.

1906
The Wounded Niobide (La Niobide blessée)
Plaster. Commissioned by the government in 1906 at the suggestion of Eugène Blot. Allocated in trust to the Musée de Bejaïa (Algeria), April 11, 1910.

Bronze. Commissioned by the government in 1907. Camille Claudel entrusted the founding using the original plaster sculpture to Eugène Blot. Allocated to the Préfecture Maritime in Toulon, September 12, 1935. Today resides in the Musée Ste.-Croix of Poitiers.

Before 1908
Bust of a Woman (Buste de femme)
Work exhibited at the Eugène Blot Gallery in 1908. A numbered series of twenty-five was made. This could be the *Countess Arthur de Maigret.*

Before 1910
Study for a Group (Étude de groupe)
Plaster. Reproduced in *L'Art décoratif,* July 1913. Disappeared.

1910
Bust of Paul Claudel at Forty-two Years of Age (Buste de Paul Claudel à quarante-deux ans)
Plaster.
Bronze. A series of six was produced by Henry Lerolle. One is in a private collection. Another has recently been acquired by the Musée Rodin from the son of Maurice Denis. Founder, Converset.

Before 1913
Self-Portrait (Autoportrait)
Plaster. Reproduced in *L'Art décoratif,* July 1913. Disappeared.

Study of a Nude (Étude de nu)
Plaster. Reproduced in *L'Art décoratif,* July 1913. Disappeared.

Head of a Negro Woman (Girl with a Chignon) (Étude de négresse)
Terra cotta. Unsigned. Private collection.
Bronze. Reproduced in *L'Art décoratif,* July 1913. Private collection.

A Note on the Casting of Camille Claudel's Work During Her Lifetime

Before 1900, Camille Claudel used the same founders as Rodin, namely Thiébaut Frères, Fumière and Gavignot, Gruet, Siot-Decauville, Converset and Alexis Rudier.

In 1900, the art critic Gustave Geffroy introduced Camille to the founder and dealer Eugène Blot, whose foundry was located at 84 rue des Archives, and his gallery at 5 Boulevard de la Madeleine. After that meeting, all of Camille Claudel's bronze works were produced by Blot. He executed a limited series, which he exhibited in his gallery in three different shows—in 1905, 1907, and 1908.

Blot's exhibition catalogs indicate contradictory and deliberately overstated series runs. His correspondence, memoirs, and the documents relating to his estate and public sales all attest to the fact that Blot thought it clever to announce castings in large numbers from the start to create the illusion of large orders. Thus, in the catalog to the 1905 exhibition, he announces the founding of *The Gossipers* in a series of fifty, while in a letter to Mathias Morhardt he specifies that the actual run was ten. Likewise, the 1905 catalog gives notice of a casting of fifty copies of *Fortune;* in his *History of a Collection,* Blot states that he limited himself to twenty copies.

During the course of public sales, the highest series number recorded was that of *The Beseecher,* No. 51. *The Waltz,* in patinated bronze, never exceeded No. 25. *The Waltz,* in gilded bronze, never exceeded a casting of two. Only a single bronze, *The Gossipers,* with screen, three *Chatelaines* lacking the founder's name (of which two are in French museums), twelve *Çacountalas,* sixteen *Fortunes* and two *Gigantis* are known to exist.

The author of this book has undertaken to inventory the series runs, which will be the topic of a catalog raisonné now in preparation.

Catalog of Exhibits

1882   Paris, Salon des Artistes Français
Old Helen. Plaster.

1883   Paris, Salon des Artistes Français
Portrait of Mme. B. Plaster.

1885   Paris, Salon des Artistes Français
Giganti. Bronze.
Old Helen. Terra cotta.

1886   Paris, Salon des Artistes Français
Bust of Louise Claudel. Bronze.

Exhibit in Nottingham

1887   Paris, Salon des Artistes Français
Young Roman (1884). Bronze.

1888   Paris, Salon des Artistes Français
Çacountala. Plaster.

1889   Paris, Salon des Artistes Français
Charles Lhermitte as a Child. Bronze.

1892   Paris, Société Nationale des Beaux-Arts
Bust of Rodin. Bronze.

Paris, Black and White Exhibit
Bust of Rodin. Bronze.

1893   Paris, Société Nationale des Beaux-Arts
The Waltz. Plaster, first version.
Clotho. Plaster.
Bust of Rodin. Bronze.

1894   Paris, Société Nationale des Beaux-Arts
The Beseecher. Plaster.
The Little Chatelaine. Bronze.

Brussels, Exposition de la Libre Esthétique
The Waltz. Bronze.
Contemplation (The Little Chatelaine?). Bronze.
Psalm. Bronze.
First Steps. Medium unknown.

1895   Paris, Société Nationale des Beaux-Arts
The Little Chatelaine. Marble, first version.
Bust of Léon Lhermitte. Bronze.
Study of a Japanese. Plaster.
The Gossipers. Plaster.

1896   Paris, Société Nationale des Beaux-Arts
The Little Chatelaine. Marble, second version.

Paris, Salon de l'Art Nouveau
Bust of Rodin. Bronze.
The Waltz. Oxidized stoneware

Geneva, Hôtel Municipal
Bust of Rodin. Bronze.

1897   Paris, Bing Gallery
Hamadryad. Marble and bronze.

Paris, Société Nationale des Beaux-Arts
The Wave. Marble and bronze.
The Gossipers. Listed as jade (actually onyx and bronze).
Countess Arthur de Maigret. Marble.

240

1898   Paris, Société Nationale des Beaux-Arts
        Hamadryad. Marble and bronze.
        Deep in Thought. Bronze.

1899   Paris, Société Nationale des Beaux-Arts
        Count Christian de Maigret in the Costume of Henri II. Marble.
        Clotho. Marble.
        Maturity. Plaster.
        Perseus and the Gorgon. Plaster, life-size.

1900   Paris, Universal Exposition
        Deep in Thought. Marble.
        Dream by the Fire. Plaster.
        Hamadryad. Marble and bronze.

        Paris, Salon de la Plume.
        Bust of Rodin. Bronze.

1902   Paris, Société Nationale des Beaux-Arts
        Perseus and the Gorgon. Marble, life-size.
        Countess Arthur de Maigret. Marble, life-size.
        The Alsatian Woman. Terra cotta.

1903   Paris, Société Nationale des Beaux-Arts
        Maturity. Bronze, second version.

1904   Paris, Second Salon d'Automne.
        Fortune. Bronze.

1905   Paris, Salon des Artistes Français
        Çacountala. Marble.
        The Flute Player. Bronze.

        Paris, Second Salon d'Automne
        Çacountala. Bronze.

        Paris, Eugène Blot Gallery
        The Beseecher. Bronze, original height.
        The Beseecher. Bronze, reduced in size.
        Perseus and the Gorgon. Bronze, reduced in size.
        Dream by the Fire. Marble.
        Fortune. Bronze.
        Intimacy. Bronze.
        Old Helen. Bronze.

The Flute Player. Bronze.
Çacountala. Bronze.
The Waltz. Bronze.
The Gossipers. Bronze.
The Gossipers. Marble.
The Wave. Onyx and bronze.

1907   Paris, Eugène Blot Gallery
Maturity. Bronze.
Bust of a Young Girl (Aurora?). Marble.

1908   Paris, Eugène Blot Gallery
Maturity. Bronze.
The Beseecher. Bronze.
Çacountala. Bronze.
The Waltz. Gilded bronze.
Aurora. Bronze.
Study of a Head for "Old Age." Bronze.
Bust of a Woman (Bust of the Countess de Maigret). Marble.
Bust of a Woman (1908). Medium unknown.
Perseus and the Gorgon. Bronze.
Fortune. Bronze.
The Little Chatelaine. Marble (1896).

1934   Paris, Le Salon des Femmes Artistes Modernes
The Beseecher. Bronze.
The Waltz. Bronze.
Bust of Rodin. Bronze.

1938   Paris, Exposition des Femmes Artistes Modernes
Bust of Rodin. Bronze.

1951   Paris, Musée Rodin, Camille Claudel Exhibition
Old Helen. Plaster.
Old Helen. Bronze.
Young Roman. Plaster (1886).
Young Roman. Bronze (1884).
Man Leaning. Plaster.
Giganti. Bronze.
Torso of a Crouching Woman. Tinted plaster.
Bust of Louise Claudel. Terra cotta.
Ferdinand de Massary. Bronze.
Bust of Rodin. Bronze.

242

Çacountala. Marble.
Çacountala. Bronze.
Çacountala. Terra cotta.
Charles Lhermitte as a Child. Bronze.
Clotho. Plaster.
The Waltz. Bronze, first version.
The Little Chatelaine. Plaster.
Aurora. Marble.
The Little Chatelaine. Marble (1895).
Bust of Léon Lhermitte. Bronze.
The Gossipers. Plaster.
The Gossipers. Onyx and bronze.
The Wave. Onyx and bronze.
Maturity. Plaster, first version.
Maturity. Bronze.
The Beseecher. Bronze.
Perseus and the Gorgon. Marble.
Perseus and the Gorgon. Bronze.
The Flute Player. Bronze.
Bust of Paul Claudel at Forty-two Years of Age. Bronze.
Fortune. Bronze.
Starving Dog. Bronze.
Head of a Negro Woman. Terra cotta.
Study of a Head. Bronze (1905).
Young Woman with a Sheaf. Terra cotta.
Study of a Head. Plaster.
Studies of Heads. Plasters (around 1885).
Study of a Head. Plaster (1897).
Man with His Arms Crossed. Terra cotta.
Blind Singer. Plaster.
Woman at Her Dressing Table. Plaster.
Louis-Prosper Claudel. Pencil.
Louise Claudel (Mme. de Massary). Pastel.

1953   Poitiers, Musée Ste.-Croix
       Çacountala. Bronze.
       The Waltz. Bronze.
       Fortune. Bronze.

1965   Paris, Paul Claudel Exhibition at the Bibliothèque Littéraire
       Jacques Doucet
       Louis-Prosper Claudel. Pencil.
       Young Roman. Bronze (1881).

Young Roman. Plaster (1886).
Paul Claudel. Colored pencil.
The Gossipers. Plaster.
The Wave. Onyx and bronze.
Çacountala. Terra cotta, two versions.
Study of a Head. Plaster (1897).
Bust of Rodin. Plaster.

1967–   Nice, Palais de la Méditerranée
1968   *The Gossipers.* Bronze.
         Maturity. Bronze.
         The Waltz. Bronze.

1968   Paris, Bibliothèque Nationale, Exhibition for the Centenary of Paul
           Claudel's Birth
         Young Roman. Tinted plaster (1886).
         Four studies of heads (see 1951 exhibition).
         Man with His Arms Crossed. Terra cotta.
         Çacountala. Marble.
         Çacountala. Terra cotta.
         Bust of Rodin. Bronze.
         Clotho. Plaster.
         The Waltz. Bronze, second version.
         The Gossipers. Plaster, without the screen.

1972   Chateauroux, Ernest Nivet Exhibition
         Young Roman. Bronze (1881).

1981   London, Bruton Gallery
         Çacountala. Bronze.

1981–   Mont-de-Marsan
1982   *Çacountala.* Marble.

1982   Lille, Musée des Beaux-Arts
         Bust of Louise Claudel. Terra cotta
         Giganti. Bronze.
         Young Roman. Bronze (1884).
         Çacountala. Bronze.

1983   Paris, Musée Rodin
         Same works as in Lille in 1982.

244

Paris, Musée National d'Art Moderne
Maturity. Bronze.

1984   Paris, Musée Rodin
Camille Claudel, February 15–June 11.

Poitiers, Musée Ste.-Croix.
Camille Claudel, June 26–September 15.

Rome, Villa Medicis.
Debussy and Symbolism, April–June.

1985   Bern, Kunstmuseum.
Camille Claudel–Auguste Rodin, March 15–May 15.

1987   Athens, French Institute of Athens.
Camille Claudel, Sculptures and Photographs, February 3–28.

Tokyo, Tokyo Art Hall.
Camille Claudel, August 28–September 16.

Sapporo (Tokyo Art Hall).
Camille Claudel, October 9–21.

Kurume, Gohibashi/Bridgestone Museum.
Camille Claudel, October 30–November 29.

Yokohama, Sogo Art Museum.
Camille Claudel, January 20–February 1.

Osaka, Daimasu Art Museum.
Camille Claudel, March 16–28.

1988   Washington, D.C., National Museum of Women in the Arts.
Camille Claudel, May 1–31.

Bibliography

Books

Bénédite, L. *Histoire des Beaux-Arts, 1800–1900*. Reference lacking.
———. *Les Sculpteurs français contemporains*. Paris: H. Laurens, 1901.
Bénézit, E. *Dictionnaire des peintres, sculpteurs, dessinateurs et graveurs*. Paris: Gründ, 1976.
Benoist, L. *Histoire de la sculpture*. Paris: Presses Universitaires de France, 1965.
———. *La Sculpture française*. Paris: Larousse, 1945 and 1963.
Blanche, J.-E. *La Vie artistique sous la IIIe République*. Paris: Editions de France, 1931.
Blot, E. *Histoire d'une collection de tableaux modernes*. Paris: Editions d'Art.
Cassar, J. *Dossier Camille Claudel*. Paris: Séguier, 1987.
Cassou, J. *Panorama des arts plastiques*. Paris: Gallimard, 1965.
Chaigne, L. *La Vie de Paul Claudel*. Tours: Mame, 1962.
Champigneulle, B. *Rodin*. Paris: Somogy, 1967.
Charmet, R. *Dictionnaire de l'art contemporain*. Paris: Larousse, 1965.
Cladel, J. *Rodin, sa vie glorieuse et inconnue*. Paris: Grasset, 1936.
Claris, E. *De l'Impressionisme en sculpture*. Paris: La Nouvelle Revue, 1902.
Claudel, P. *Correspondance avec André Gide (1899–1926)*. Paris: Gallimard, 1949.
———. *Correspondance avec Francis Jammes et Gabriel Frizeau (1897–1938)*. Paris: Gallimard, 1952.

246

————. *Journal,* vols. 1 *(1904–1932) and* 2 *(1933–1955).* Paris: Gallimard, "Bibliothèque de la Pléiade," 1968 and 1969.

————. *Mémoires improvisés.* Paris: Gallimard, 1969.

————. *Oeuvres en prose.* Paris: Gallimard, "Bibliothèque de la Pléiade," 1969.

Daudet, L. *Fantômes et vivants.* Paris: Nouvelle Librairie Nationale, 1914.

————. *La Vie orageuse de Clemenceau.* Paris: Albin Michel, 1938.

Descharnes, R., and J.-F. Chabrun. *Auguste Rodin.* Paris: Bibliothèque des Arts, 1967.

Elsen, A. *Rodin's* Gates of Hell. Minneapolis: Minnesota University Press, 1960.

Fontainas, A., and L. Vauxcelles. *Histoire générale de l'art français de la Révolution à nos jours,* vol. 2. Paris: Librairie de France, 1925.

Frisch, V., and J. Schipley. *Auguste Rodin: A Biography.* New York: Frederick A. Stokes and Co., 1939.

Gischia, L., and N. Vedrès. *La Sculpture en France depuis Rodin.* Paris: Seuil, 1954.

Goncourt, E. and J. de. *Journal: Mémoires de la vie littéraire et artistique.* 4 vols. Paris: Flammarion, 1959.

Gsell, P. *Auguste Rodin. L'Art.* Conversations collected by Paul Gsell. Paris: Grasset, 1911.

Guillemin, H. *Le Converti Paul Claudel.* Paris: Gallimard, 1968.

Histoire de l'art. Published under the direction of Bernard Dorival. Paris: Gallimard, "Encyclopédie de la Pléiade," 1969.

Jianou, I. *Rodin.* Paris: Arted, 1980.

Lami, S. *Dictionnaire des sculpteurs de l'école française du XIXe siècle.* Paris: Champion, 1921.

Lethève, J. *La Vie quotidienne des artistes français au XIXe siècle.* Paris: Hachette, 1968.

Letourneur, R. *La Sculpture française contemporaine.* Monaco: Les Documents d'art, 1944.

Lockspeiser, E. *Claude Debussy.* Paris: Fayard, 1980.

Maillard, L. *Auguste Rodin, statuaire.* Paris: H. Floury, 1899.

Martinie, A.-H. *Histoire générale de l'art,* vol. 4. 1938.

Mondor, H. *Claudel plus intime.* Paris: Gallimard, 1960.

Read, H. *A Concise History of Modern Sculpture.* London: Thames & Hudson, 1964.

Renard, J. *Journal.* Paris: Gallimard, "Bibliothèque de la Pléiade," 1967.

Rivière, A. *L'Interdite.* Paris: Tierce, 1983.

Rudel, J. *Technique de la sculpture.* Paris: Presses Universitaires de la France, 1980.

Selz, J. *Découverte de la sculpture moderne.* Lausanne: Les Fausonnières et La Guilde, 1963.

Tancock, J.-L. *The Sculpture of Auguste Rodin.* Philadelphia: Museum of Art, 1976.

Thieme, U., and F. Becker. *Allgemeines Lexikon der Bildenden Kunstler von der Antike bis zur Gegenwart,* vol. 7. Leipzig: W. Engelmann, 1907–1947.

Varillon, E. *Claudel.* Paris: Desclée de Brouwer, "Les Ecrivains devant Dieu," 1967.

Articles

Asselin, H. "Camille Claudel et les sirènes de la sculpture." *La Revue française* (April 1966): 8.

———. "La Vie douloureuse de Camille Claudel, sculpteur." Typescript of two programs for the Radio Télévision Française, 1956. Claudel bequest, Bibliothèque Nationale.

Bielinky, J. "Le Salon des femmes artistes modernes." Unattached press clipping. June 24, 1934.

Bouchot, H. "Le Salon de 1893." *Gazette des Beaux-Arts.* 48: 118.

Bourdeau, L. "Les Salons." *Revue encyclopédique Larousse* (1893): 823.

Braisne, H. de. "Camille Claudel." *La Revue idéaliste,* no. 19 (October 19, 1897).

Bulletin de la Société Paul Claudel, no. 32, 37, 45.

Claudel, C. "Boîte aux lettres." *L'Europe artiste* (May 28, 1899).

Claudel, P. "Camille Claudel statuaire." *L'Occident* (August 1905). Text reprinted in *L'Art décoratif* (July–December 1913) and in *L'Oeil écoute, Oeuvres en prose* (Paris: Gallimard, 1969): 272.

———. "Ma soeur Camille." Text written for the Camille Claudel Exhibit at the Musée Rodin in November–December 1951. It served as the preface to the catalog. Published in *Oeuvres en prose,* op. cit., 276.

Cochin, H. "Salon de 1903." *Gazette des Beaux-Arts.* Unattached clipping.

Desjardins, P. "Les Salons de 1899." Sixth and last article in series. *Gazette des Beaux-Arts* (2nd semester, 1899): 283–292.

Espiau de La Maestre, A. "L'Annonce faite à Marie." *Les Lettres romanes,* Université Catholique de Louvain, no. 1 (1962): 3–26; no. 2: 149–171; no. 3: 241–265.

Fagus, F. "Le Salon de la Nationale." *Revue blanche* (May 15, 1899).

"La Femme moderne par elle-même." *Revue encyclopédique Larousse* (November 1896). Unsigned article.

Fermigier, A. "Itinéraire estival de St.-Tropez à Calais." *Le Monde* (July 31, 1975).

Fontainas, A. "Les Salons de 1899." *Mercure de France,* no. 114. Unattached clipping.

Fourcaud, L. "La Sculpture à la Société Nationale des Beaux-Arts." *Revue des arts décoratifs,* vol. 19 (1899): 247–257.

Geffroy, G. "Çacountala." *Le Journal* (December 15, 1895).

248

————. *Revue de Paris* (3rd trimester, 1895): 428–448.

————. *La Vie artistique* (1893): 337; (1894): 380; (1895): 147–224; (1900): 349–432; (1901): 291.

Gelber, L. "Camille Claudel's Art and Influences." *Claudel Studies*, vol. 1, no. 1 (1972): 36–43.

Ginepro, J. "L'Apothéose de Rodin." *L'Estampille* (January 1983).

Gsell, P. "L'Esprit féminin dans les Beaux-Arts." *La Revue* (March 15, 1904).

Guillemin, H. "Claudel jusqu'à sa conversion." *La Revue de Paris* (1955).

Hamel, M. "Les Salons de 1905." *Revue de Paris*.

Jakenski. *La Vie Parisienne* (October 1904).

Kahn, G. "Au jour le jour." *Le Siècle* (December 29, 1905).

Leroi, P. "Le Salon de 1886." *L'Art*. Unattached clipping.

————. "Le Salon de 1888." *L'Art*. Unattached clipping.

Marcel, H. "Les Salons de 1902." *Gazette des Beaux-Arts*. Unattached clipping.

Marx, R. "Le Salon de 1895." *Gazette des Beaux-Arts*. Unattached clipping.

Mauclair, C. "L'Art des femmes peintres et sculpteurs en France." *La Revue des revues* (4th trimester, 1901): 523–525.

Michel, A. "Promenades aux Salons." Feuilleton of the *Journal des débats* (May 12, 1903).

Mirbeau, O. "Ça et là." *Le Journal, quotidien littéraire, artistique et politique* (May 12, 1895).

Monod, F. "L'Exposition de Mlle. Camille Claudel et de M. Bernard Hoetger." *Art et décoration*, supplement (January 1906).

Morand, E. "Le Salon de 1905." *Gazette des Beaux-Arts*. Unattached clipping.

Morhardt, M. "Mlle. Camille Claudel." *Mercure de France* (March 1898).

————. "Sur un marbre disparu de Camille Claudel." *Le Temps* (September 14, 1935).

Morice, C. "Le Salon d'Automne." *Mercure de France* (December 1905): 376–396.

Myra, A. *Le Petit quotidien* (December 11, 1905).

Natanson, T. "Notes sur les Salons." *Revue blanche* (June 1, 1898).

Pictor. "Les Salons." *Le Monde élégant* (May 17, 1893).

Pilon, G. "Camille Claudel." *Iris* (June 1900).

Pingeot, A. "Le Chef-d'oeuvre de Camille Claudel: l'Age Mûr." *La Revue du Louvre et des Musées de France*, no. 4 (October 1982): 292–295.

Pottier, E. "Le Salon de 1892." *Gazette des Beaux-Arts*, 46: 34.

Rolland, R. "Les Salons de 1903." *La Revue de Paris* (June 1, 1903): 664.

Salmon, A. "Les Femmes et l'art." *Aux Ecoutes* (August 28, 1937).

Sertat, R. *Revue encyclopédique Larousse* (1892): 1261.

Silvestre, A. "La Vague. La Sculpture aux salons de 1897." *Gazette des Beaux-Arts*. Unattached clipping.

Vauxcelles, L. "A propos de Camille Claudel. Quelques oeuvres d'une grande artiste inconnue du public." *Gil Blas* (July 10, 1913).

———. "Lettres et arts." *La Volonté* (August 1, 1932).
La Vie (October 4, and November 1, 1913). Photographs.
de Wyzewa, T. "Le Salon de 1894." *Gazette des Beaux-Arts*, 50: 34.

Catalogs

1905: *Exposition d'oeuvres de Camille Claudel et de Bernard Hoetger du 4 décembre au 16 décembre*. Galérie Eugène Blot.

1907: *Exposition de sculptures nouvelles par Camille Claudel et de peintures par Manguin, Marquet, Puy, du 24 octobre au 10 novembre*. Galérie Eugène Blot.

1908: *Exposition de Mesdames Camille Claudel, Gaston Devore, Jeanne Eliot, Alcide Lebeau, Hassenberg, Ann Osterlind, du 1er au 24 décembre*. Galérie Eugène Blot.

1938: *Catalogue du Musée Rodin*. Paris: Georges Grappe.

1951: *Catalogue de l'exposition Camille Claudel*. Musée Rodin.

1965: *Catalogue de l'exposition Paul Claudel*. Bibliothèque Littéraire Jacques Doucet.

1968: *Catalogue de l'exposition pour le centenaire de la naissance de Paul Claudel*. Bibliothèque Nationale.

1984: *Catalogue de l'exposition Camille Claudel*. Musée Rodin.
Debussy e il simbolismo. Villa Medici. Rome: Filli Palombi Editori.

1985: *Catalogue de l'exposition Camille Claudel–Auguste Rodin*. Kunstmuseum. Berne: Musée des Beaux-Arts de Berne/Office du Livre de Fribourg.

1987: *Catalogue de l'exposition Camille Claudel*. Institut Français d'Athènes.
Camille Claudel in Japan: A Catalog of the Exhibit. Asahi Shimbun.

Archives

Archives Nationales (France).
Archives du Musée Rodin.
Fonds Camille Claudel. Bibliothèque Nationale.
Fonds Paul Claudel. Bibliothèque Nationale.
Société des Manuscrits des Auteurs Français. Bibliothèque Nationale.

Index

251